Tales from the
Emergency Room

Tales from the Emergency Room

Remembrances from a Life in Medicine

William E. Hermance, MD, FAAAAI

"I have to push because you won't get out of the way when I shout!"

To order additional copies of this book, contact:
Xlibris Corporation
1-888-795-4274
www.Xlibris.com
Orders@Xlibris.com
68040

Table of Contents

Introduction 9

The Early Years.. 11

The El-Hi Years 13

The College Years 20

The Medical School Years.. 30

The Post-Graduate Training Years 53

The Military Years.. 78

The Practice Years 93

    In the Office.. 93

    In the Clinic 153

The Retirement Years 158

Miscellaneous 166

Reflections 174

Dedication

For Peggy,

who heard these stories when they first occurred and so
many times since, that she could easily have
written them down all by herself!

Special Appreciation to:

Patricia Stiller Hermance

George W. Hermance

Introduction

In the emergency room where I trained, there were several levels of activity. Slow (rare), busy (normal), hectic (often) and busy-hectic (the worst!). From a visitor's point of view, "chaotic" would have appeared to be a good choice to describe the scenes. It was never that way for the doctors, nurses and medical/surgical assistants, for every move was purposeful, undertaken to achieve an acceptable medical outcome.

I did my post-medical school training at The Roosevelt Hospital in New York City in Manhattan. It was and still is one of the premier teaching hospitals in the country. It has been affiliated over the years with the finest medical institutions in the world. It is called St. Luke's-Roosevelt Hospital Center now. I started my practice just as Medicare and Medicaid began. Training after college lasted eight years including medical school, interrupted by two years of Selective Service Duty. During my career, there were great happiness and satisfaction, times of joy and sadness and lots of laughs. I noticed early on that almost everybody enjoyed hearing medical tales. I also learned very quickly, as all medical personnel should, that specific medical facts about patients were not to be shared with anyone not directly involved in the patient's care. Not in the lunch room, the elevator, the waiting room or any place where casual observers might overhear. But, so many interesting or humorous situations occurred that could be told without giving a clue to a patient's identity, that repeating them here seems acceptable.

My youngest son is a police officer. I suggested that he keep a journal of the interesting things that happen to him in the course of his work since he does tell wonderful stories about his adventures on the police force. But he, like me, hasn't done it. So perhaps when he is retired he will decide to record those memories as I am doing here.

I spoke the subtitle above one day in the busy, crowded emergency room. I had to nudge a woman out of my way after indicating out loud that she should move so that I could get to where I was needed. She asked why I had "pushed" her and I said, my voice rising, "I have to push because you won't get out of the way when I shout." Those words seemed to me upon later reflection to describe the tone of many medical venues especially on "hectic" days.

Not all of these stories originate out of the emergency room. But it is not difficult to decide from what locale they do come. I have left out names purposely except in a few instances where they are important or I especially wanted to make note of specific people.

Finally, to quote a local Emergency Room doctor, appearing utterly shocked when I asked for directions to the Recovery Room, "Somebody recovered here?!"

The Early Years

Vegetable Soup

Of course, I don't remember when I decided to become a doctor. I think it was a gradual process, but as far as I can remember, that is always what I have wanted to do. One family story, though, has it that I told my grandmother one day while visiting the family farm when I was about five or six years old, that I wanted to raise vegetable soup when I grew up. An ambition that I never realized.

The Chain Letter

In the days before I was born, chain letters were not illegal. My father had entered a letter containing $1.00 in one of these schemes. The cost of my delivery was $300.00 and on the very day that I was born, he received 300 letters in the mail each containing $1.00. I often mention this stroke of good fortune when discussing the cost of medical care!

A Nail-Biter

As a young boy I was a nail-biter. I guess I switched to that after I stopped sucking my thumb! My first and best friend growing up lived next-door to me, but then moved several blocks away. By that time we were riding our bikes all over so we continued to be good buddies. His mother had a dear friend who worked for the local dermatologist with whom I had some dealings (warts), mostly with unpleasant and long-lasting ill effects (but that is another story). Frequently, when I went to my friend's house, his mother's lady friend would be there. She would always insist on examining my fingernails and then read me the riot act because I continued to bite them. It got so that if I saw her car I would try to get my buddy's attention without alerting the ogre. I can't tell you what anxiety this woman provoked in me. Looking back, I believe that this was a form of abuse. And, of course, I would see her in the doctor's office when my parents took me there. Naturally, I eventually stopped the nail-biting, but it was not because of the anxiety this woman instilled in me.

College?

It never occurred to me that one could not go to college. I remember playing with some friends when I was about thirteen while they had some older cousins visiting. One of the older boys noted that he was not going to college and another said that he wasn't either but would be going to work soon, just out of high school. I couldn't wait to report this to my parents, both college educated, only to find out that, yes, indeed, one did not have to go to college! Who knew?

The Dentist

Even though I have several friends who are dentists, one of whom was my dentist for many years, I have always looked forward with dread to a dentist appointment. A possible reason for this was the dentist my parents and my friends' parents sent us to. I was there frequently since I had awful teeth as did my friends. (Fluoridation hadn't been invented yet.) It turned out that this man never used local anesthesia with us kids although he did with our parents. I can remember vividly being treated by him as can some of my long-time friends. One of these and I still cringe even while we are laughing about our early dental encounters.

The El-Hi Years

Gover(n)ment

In the sixth grade, my teacher asked me to stay behind after school one day. I knew this lady very well since she and her husband were my parents' best friends. My father was by then involved in the politics of education as was my teacher. It seems that I had misspelled "government" on my most recent spelling test. In a note to my teacher my father had made the same mistake. Exasperated, she had me write "government" 100 times on the blackboard. It took a long time but I did it, and, just as this teacher knew, never again did I misspell that word. I never heard about it from my father either though I am sure he was not unaware of the episode.

Sometime later because of an attitude the same sixth grade teacher thought I was developing, she again asked me to stay after school. This time she made a prediction, self-fulfilling or not I don't know. She allowed that I was at the head of my class, but that when I got to high school (10th grade in those days) I would find that the academic competition was greater and I would not be at the very top of things. Then she said that in college I would encounter the same problem. And then the prediction: Billy would graduate in the middle of his class in medical school. How she knew all this was a mystery to me then as now, but her prediction turned out to be exactly right.

Handwriting

My mother and father were both school teachers. One day I handed my father an assignment which I had done for school. The work was fine, he said but he had some advice for me. My handwriting, though legible enough, was very small. His idea was for me to practice writing larger and in that way I would fill up more space on assignments. So, I practiced making my script larger. In school in the future, I would sometimes think how much more impressive the amount of writing I produced looked when written large.

Then there was the teaching assistant in my college physics course who was charged with evaluating everyone's lab reports. By that time, my penmanship had also improved to the point where it looked quite nice, but was sometimes difficult to read because of its regular quality. My TA called me aside one day and asked if he could prevail upon me to type my reports. He said that he had to leave my reports till last because he got seasick reading them. In the hope that he wouldn't read them at all, I continued to write the papers in longhand.

Seventh Grade Revisited

Our history teacher in 7th grade social studies was very strict and gave enormous amounts of homework. Because of this, I was prevailed upon by my classmates to lead a delegation to the principal to register our complaint. It never crossed my mind that my father, well-known in the school system, would find out about this almost instantaneously. I had not mentioned our efforts at home. Thinking back, I don't remember any serious consequences either for the teacher or for us students, but I do remember another teacher whom I knew personally saying to me that with regard to homework in high school and college I hadn't seen anything yet.

About 25 years later I received a phone call in my office from this lady. I had no trouble remembering who she was. She had come upon bad times with regard to her health and possibly her income, and, having kept track of my career, called to see if I could be of assistance. I was able to help her in a small way by sending her to one of the leading internists in town, who, at my request agreed to care for her with no fee and to guide her to some social assistance. (He had been in 7th grade when I was, but in a different elementary school in town.) I was happy to be able to assuage my conscience somewhat since I had always felt rather badly about the way I and the rest of my class had treated her.

I Love My Job

My very first job was with an old gentleman civil engineer. He was a bachelor and lived in a very old and dingy house. This is where I worked when I was not out in the field with him. He wasn't unkind to me but my working conditions were abysmal. When I decided to quit, it was with some trepidation since a friend of my father's had been instrumental in finding the work for me. I also decided that I would never have another job that I didn't want to wake up to every morning even if that meant going on public assistance. My father was not nearly as put out as I thought he would be when I quit. I never worked at a job I didn't love again. I was always happy to get to the office in the morning because I knew my day would be filled with interesting people and interesting problems. Even now, back working in my specialty, I love what I am doing.

Dr. Nash

For three years in high school and college I worked in one of our town's leading pharmacies. The proprietor, tall and good-looking, decided every year when it came time for me to go back to school, that I was the cause of him losing a lot of money. (I wasn't of course and he kept rehiring me in the summers.) His wife became pregnant for the first time and went into labor. As she was going up in the elevator at the hospital, the nun asked her if this was her first baby. Her reply? "No, my last!" She subsequently did have another baby.

Three Fingers

One evening, I found myself alone in the pharmacy. A young man came up to the prescription counter and pressed three fingers of his right hand into the palm of his left hand and lightly tapped them into his palm three times.

He spoke not a word. I was totally mystified. To one side of the counter was an elegant set of wooden built-in drawers each with a small brass frame into which a card was inserted bearing a list of the contents of the drawer. I glanced in that direction and noticed that one of the labels was not black and white typing, but red and white with no words. Aha, I said to myself, Trojan condoms come in red and white packages of three. Having no idea if I was right, I removed a three pack from the drawer and put it on the counter. The man laid his fifty cents down, picked up the condoms and left. No one was around to witness this transaction and a similar one never occurred to me again. To this day, I am rather proud of myself for figuring out the sign language. Those days are far removed now when enormous displays of condoms adorn drugstore walls.

The Orderly

When I was in high school and college, I worked as an orderly at St. Agnes Hospital in White Plains, NY. I was born there and subsequently my daughter was born there as well. I always worked the night shift so that I would be able to spend my days with my friends, often on weekends at the beach. So, I would get off early on Friday morning, sleep a short time and then catch up with the gang. By Friday night I wasn't able to sleep very well since that was my usual working time. But, Saturday was always a busy time, too. Late parties on Saturday night were the best since I would be wide awake. On Sunday evening, I would arrive at the hospital pretty much wiped out. I endeavored to complete my duties in a timely fashion so I could have a nap (on company time I must confess). I worked on the main medical floor for the "charge nurse". We all called each other by our last names only and enjoyed working together. Some nights if it was slow I would have a rest on an unused gurney. When I woke up, I was often in an entirely different location having been wheeled there by my "friends". Once, I was presented with an oblong, pink cellophane bag tied at one end with a blue ribbon. This was a symbol of the many times I had prepared male patients for surgery. I was also fired three times by the head nun on our floor, probably because I was having too much fun. The head Sister of the hospital always hired me back in the morning. Indeed, eventually no one was able to make up a hospital bed better or faster than I, a real achievement among the pros. Many years later it was my privilege as a doctor and an old friend to wish my charge nurse the very best upon her retirement from nursing.

The Glasses

When I was sixteen years old, I went to New York City on a class trip to the opera (Lucia di Lammermoor). I was seated on the train with my best friend, Lou, who commented about one of the advertising signs at the end of the rail car. Well, to my amazement and Lou's amusement, I was unable to make out the writing on the sign.

I told my parents about this and my father and I went off to the ophthalmologist. After my exam, as the doctor was writing out the prescription for my glasses, I noticed that he reached into his desk drawer and took a drink out of a soda bottle. After I got my new glasses, I had a great deal of trouble figuring out where my feet should be. I tripped up stairs and nearly fell downstairs several times. I thought that this was just me getting used to the glasses but finally, I had to report the problem. My father then took me to see an optometrist friend of his. This doctor reported that, while the ophthalmologist had gotten the prescription correct, he had written it upside down—or something like that. The lenses were corrected and ever since I have worn glasses quite comfortably.

The ophthalmologist in question turned out to be an alcoholic, drinking straight whiskey out of his soda bottle. He soon closed his practice and after a lengthy time successfully reopened it having become a recovering alcoholic.

A Platonic Friend

In high school I was a member of the foreign exchange student club. We met with other clubs from nearby schools and got to know visiting students. There I met a pretty young lady and we became good friends. (She would eventually introduce me to her best friend who later became my wife. She figures in a later story.) We had a purely platonic relationship but would call one another up and get together if neither of us was otherwise occupied. One summer night I returned my "date" to her house quite late and she sat on her brick front steps while I stood as we chatted a bit more. Then I said that I was leaving, expecting her to go into her house. When she didn't budge after much coaxing, I just left her there, checking to see that she actually did go inside as I drove off. It seems that we had had a good laugh or two after we got to her house. She wet her pants and knew that that would be obvious when she stood up. What a good sport she was to tell me about her problem later on. She is still a good sport and a good friend.

The Hat

In an OB-GYN class in medical school we had all convened on schedule but no professor showed up so we all left. The professor was not happy, but it reminded me of a story about my father when I was about seven years old. He often took night courses at New York University in the City and so I was used to his routine. One night he came home before I had gone to bed. Most unusual on his class night. Two weeks later I remember him rummaging around in the closet for an old fedora. He left with it and once again returned early.

Two weeks before, his class of adults had shown up but the professor did not, though his hat was on his desk. So, after an appropriate waiting period, the class left. The next week a very annoyed professor announced that, "When my hat is here, I'm here!" Before the next class all the students arrived a bit early, placed a hat on their desks and left. The professor never said another word about his hat and thereafter showed up on time to teach, albeit with some catching up to do in the curriculum.

Sundays with Hilara

A few houses down the hill from my house a neighbor lady ran a lending library. My mother had to be her best customer. Hilara was a speed reader and so she went through books at a rapid pace. She did a lot of her reading on Sunday afternoons and my friends would often gather around to question her about what she had read while slowly, steadily turning the pages of a book. Their skepticism about her ability was allayed after they had carefully perused the pages she was reading and she had gotten everything right. To this day my friends remember my mother, probably because she did not seem to realize what a significant ability she had.

Also, when I was very young, my mother and I would go to the paper store across the street from church. It never failed that we would be surrounded by some very unusual people. They certainly did not fit my definition of "normal". It was obvious that they loved my mother. Later, I found out that she had been the first special education teacher in the school system, before the days when these mentally and physically challenged people were "mainlined". So, Hilara would go to their homes to teach them, probably the only educational help they had ever gotten, and they had not forgotten their gratitude for my mother.

The College Years

The Valedictorian

Shortly after I arrived on campus at college I was wandering around wearing my Frosh beanie as required, when two other freshmen approached and we started up a conversation. Eventually, one of the guys noted that he had been valedictorian of his high school class. I asked how many were in his class. There were 46. His companion had the distinction of being salutatorian of his class of 23. I couldn't resist and so I said, quite truthfully, "There were 643 people in my graduating class." And I walked off. Let them wonder about my high school class rank, I thought.

Cutthroats

It wasn't long after I got to college that I learned about cutthroats. They were plentiful among the pre-med students. It was said that they would stoop to anything to see if other people's scores on tests and projects were above or below theirs. There may actually have been attempts to change results or mislead others into poorer performances, but that, thankfully, did not happen to me. My group of pre-med friends was highly supportive of each other, even tutoring one another on occasion. However, it was not unusual for me to be informed of my scores on tests while on my way across campus before I even got to the postings. I remember one man who actually studied with a gun displayed on his desk—a friend of mine took me to see for myself. My feeling was that the people who spent their time creating and maintaining lists of students they were in "competition" with might better have used their time in academic study. In any case, several of the cutthroats were eventually unable to get into medical school. Almost everyone in my group was accepted at their medical school of choice. In fact, seven of the eight who applied to the University of Rochester School of Medicine and Dentistry were accepted there in spite of a policy of the medical school to accept only about three students from its own college class. The eighth studied elsewhere. (We all felt a little uncomfortable about that, but he wound up at an excellent school as well.)

Speech Training

Included in our first semester of college was a course, mandatory for all, in speech training. There were weekly critiques of our use of the English language. The thing about it all that I remember best, probably because I got kidded about it so much, was the professor's admonition to me that I must learn to speak in a lower register. While saying this she forced her voice into the baritone range. I went about trying to train myself to do this, usually when my roommate was present, but I never did succeed. We had a lot of laughs about it though.

Big Brother

Upon arrival in college I was assigned a "big brother" who was a senior in pre-med. I really do not know how I would have made it without him. Despite my successful high school career, I was unprepared for college study. I like to say that my big brother dragged me kicking and screaming through my freshman year. By the time he went off to medical school I was able to get along on my own. I am forever grateful for his advice and counsel.

About ten years later I attended a medical staff meeting at Lenox Hill Hospital in New York where I was an attending physician. The new Director of Hematology was introduced during the meeting. He was my old friend! As the meeting ended and I made my way toward him, he turned, looked at me and said, "Hi Bill!" Subsequently he sent patients to me and we worked together on fund-raising projects for The University of Rochester. It was a real pleasure to become reacquainted with my college mentor.

Bibs

Not long after college classes began I met a girl named Bibs. I have no idea if this is her actual given name or not. However, we saw each other frequently, mostly lounging around the student union. We might even have had a date or two. One day while we were sitting in the lounge Bibs remarked to me that she had finally figured out what my "line" was. I had only a vague idea of what this might mean. She announced that my "line" was that I didn't have a "line". I guessed that she was right. Anyway, we had a lot of fun together. In one noteworthy instance, we had carefully coordinated our train ride back to school after Thanksgiving break. I got on the train at Harmon station and she got on at Albany. (Bibs was heiress to a well known household cleanser fortune located near Albany, a fact I did not find out about until much later.) In those days, one could smoke on the train and so we did. Bibs carried a small silver silent butler in her purse into which she deposited her cigarette ashes. Near Utica I began to smell something burning and then several others did, too. Of course, it was Bib's purse, not quite in flames yet, but certainly on fire. The silent butler had come open and spilled smoldering ashes. After much commotion and things were back under control, we had a good laugh. I have never seen any such thing as that little device since then.

The Cigarette

In my freshman year at college, a friend who owned a car suggested that four of us drive to New York City with him. I agreed to go if I could be left off in White Plains where, I assured everyone, my mother would have plenty of refreshments for us before the rest of the group continued on. I cautioned my travelling companions quite emphatically not to mention that I smoked. While we were enjoying our supper at my parents' house, my father, in an apparent attempt to say that I was now allowed to smoke, offered me a cigarette. A chorus of voices rang out, "Oh, Bill doesn't smoke!" I knew my father instantly realized what had happened and so I accepted the cigarette, able now to smoke without guilt.

Assorted Ice Creams

My father was in Syracuse, NY on business and invited me and my roommate George to meet him at his hotel for dinner. It was not a long drive and a half-way decent free meal appealed to us. When the dessert menu was presented to us, my father's brilliant son ordered the "assorted ice creams". My roommate didn't even try to let this go unnoticed and so we both burst out laughing. My father smiled indulgently probably wondering how he had wound up with these two nuts!

That was not the only time he and I managed to attract attention over something we found hilarious. A notable example occurred just before my friend died as we were walking with our wives through an antique shop in Mt. Dora, Florida. We both spotted a yellow china cup labeled "yellow cup". Our wives shooed us onto the street where we continued our uproarious laughing sitting on a curbside bench.

The Dead Cat

I have mentioned the girl who was my occasional date in a previous story. We were pals, buddies. In our group we used to play practical jokes on one another and the crowd would assign points for whatever mischief we managed to pull off. One evening at Christmastime, we went out dancing as a group. The dance floor was extremely crowded. I asked Margie to dance and arranged for her to precede me onto the dance floor. I suggested that she move right into the center of the crowd. Then I returned to my table and waited with the rest of the group to see what would happen. Naturally, when she turned around, already in dance position, I was nowhere to be seen. By the time she got back to the table, the crowd was laughing. My friend cheerfully agreed that she had been had. I would pay, I knew, but I did get a lot of points.

On Valentine's Day the following year, I went to pick up my mail at the college post office where a rather large package was waiting for me. It did not have a return address, but in those days, that was of no consequence. Back in the dormitory I opened the package and discovered a quite thoroughly dissected cat. I knew instantly that it was from Margie who was in Miami, Ohio studying to be pharmacist and was taking vertebrate anatomy as I was in Rochester. For some weeks thereafter, I occasionally used the cat specimen to study in my room. The cleaning lady dutifully shifted the box back and forth under the sink as she went about her work. (I'm quite sure she knew what was in the box.) Of course, my friend won all the points there were to win and remains far ahead of me in that regard to this day. All of our friends were highly entertained. (I had the honor to introduce Margie to the assembled multitude at our Fiftieth Wedding Anniversary party as the reason we were all there, since she had introduced Peggy and me.)

The Mouse-brown Limousine

In 1953, my father and I bought a used Dodge 4-door with fluid drive. Since the car had belonged to a good friend of his and since my father taught auto mechanics in high school, we knew the car was in excellent condition. It was a significant $300.00 investment for me, however, and I took very good care of the car. My college friends rode all over with me but they knew the rules, such as no eating in the car, and they abided by them. Later on, as an engagement present, my parents presented us with a case of motor oil. For our wedding present my father had the engine entirely rebuilt. Both of these strange gifts would eventually save us a lot of money.

After I was married as a sophomore in medical school we continued to drive the car. However, the car was the same color as the street outside our apartment and was hardly visible from our garret apartment. It really was a mouse-brown color. At some point the glove compartment door could not be closed and stuck straight out over the passenger's knees. Add to this a completely rusted away floor on the passenger side due to Rochester winter road salt. Thus, riding in the car was an adventure. Our baby sitters, who were nursing school students, knew to ride with one foot on the frame and the other on the drive shaft, and not to look down. They also gave up trying to close the glove compartment door.

When medical school graduation weekend arrived, my father, thinking mainly about his grandson, announced that we would not be riding home in that car. So, we took it to the nearby junk yard and sold it for $35.00. It had served us well for 7 years and provided us with many stories and fond memories.

The GI Bug

At times, my best college friend could be very precise. In our sophomore year an epidemic of food poisoning swept the campus. I was spared because I had not eaten the tainted food, but nearly everyone else had. I knew my former roommate was sick, so I decided to visit him in his room directly above mine. When I entered his room, it was plain that he had been really sick. He said to me as I stood there in my crepe soled shoes, "It may interest you to know that you are standing in my shit." It did indeed interest me and I retreated to the hall. Whereupon he arose from his sick bed, bundled up all the bed clothes and marched naked to the incinerator chute. So, I knew he was getting better and left him to finish the cleanup. Over the years, I would still chide George about throwing all that bedding and clothes out.

Contraband Liquor

These days especially it is not prudent to be smart with border officers. But, neither was it back in 1956, in the middle of the night when the officers had little to do. My college friend and eventual medical school roommate, Chuck, our girl friends (who both became our wives) and his parents had spent several days in the Michigan north woods at his parents' cabin. We were on our way back to Rochester by the shortest route, through Canada, when we crossed the border in the middle of the night. Peggy and I were travelling in my car behind the others. Chuck's mother had a fun-loving disposition, was a known jokester and went by the name "Hotrod Hannah" in some circles because of her driving style. We noted that their car had been directed to pull into a slot by the station house, and then, we were directed there, too. We got out of my car and were herded into the station. We were questioned about what we might be transporting into the States and were told our car was about to be examined. Now, these officers had virtually nothing to do as far as we could see and they could plainly tell that we were just "innocent" college students. But, search the car they did, finding nothing suspicious. Eventually, we were allowed to proceed on our way. It seems that when our host and his folks had been cleared at the border, his mother announced that she had reason to believe that the car behind them was carrying contraband liquor. Thus, the inspection procedure. We spent an hour there and I am not sure that Hotrod was having as much fun as she thought she would. Despite that we have laughed about the episode for many years.

A Messy College Room

My college roommate and I kept a very neat dormitory room. His mother used to mail his personal laundry to him—ironed sheets and underwear—which stunned me. But we rarely had a mess in our room, beds were made, clothes hung up, etc. One day however we were both being a bit sloppy and the room was in maximum disarray, looking like a bombsite. My roommate's mother and father showed up unannounced. I knew who it was of course, but I continued to fake a nap, facing the wall, while George's father opened the windows to air the place out and his mother began straightening things up. It was a most unpleasant visit for us both, the more so since I steadfastly refused to become involved. Later we often laughed about his parents' visit on one of the few days when things were not "just so".

Dr. Engel's Mail

My college roommate and best friend had the same name as an internationally renowned psychiatrist and eventual professor of mine at the medical school. When we went to pick up our mail I would often watch him sort through his mail and toss letter after letter into the trash. George was throwing away all of the doctor's mail which had come to him. This went on for the whole time we were in college. Years later at my twentieth medical school reunion I had a chance to talk with the psychiatrist who by then was well into his eighties. I knew he would have no idea who I was, but I told him the story of the mail mix up. He paused and then said that at one time, for several years, he had received very little mail and had never been able to figure out why. I was glad to be able to enlighten him—a role reversal of sorts.

Medical School Interviews

Midway through our junior year in college we began our medical school applications. These nearly always required personal interviews at the schools we had applied to. It was easy to get to my interviews at the University of Rochester Medical School since it was just a short walk across the college campus. My close friend and confidant and early medical school roommate, Chuck, and I had one of our interviews with the same young doctor at the medical school. At the end of my interview, the doctor asked me if I knew Chuck. Startled, I said that I did. He said that he thought so since my answers to his questions were virtually identical with Chuck's. I admitted the closeness of our relationship and the fact that he and I discussed everything of importance with one another. Of course, I decided on the spot that neither one of us would be accepted at Rochester.

As if that weren't enough, my second interview was with a Nobel Laureate. Someone had given me a subscription to Scientific American and, by chance, I had begun to read an article in the magazine on the Theory of Numbers. To be honest, I paid attention to the summary of the article just under the title and little else, since it was all way beyond me. The professor greeted me cordially and asked a few questions about myself. Then he paused, looked me in the eye and said, "What do you know about the Theory of Numbers?" I recited what I had read of the article, whereupon he proceeded to regale me with a long and complicated explanation of the theory. My job, I guessed, was to listen and keep looking as intelligent as I could. Again I thought that my goose was cooked as far as the U of R medical school was concerned.

My friend and I were accepted at the medical school, first choice for both of us. To this day, I think that there must have been other reasons for the school to accept me and that I might have missed the purpose of the interviews altogether.

Another Medical School Interview

I arranged an appointment for an interview at a well-known Boston medical school. I was aware that new rules applied to such interviews, namely that the applicant would not be told whether or not he/she was accepted, at the interview. So, off I went on my first plane ride, in the pouring rain. The Chairman of the Anatomy Department was to interview me. We met in the student snack room. The Chairman turned out to be a woman. Her opening line was about the fact that she hadn't known what to expect I would look like since I had not sent a picture with my application. (I am sure that I did!) Then she began to ask a few questions, one of which I remember clearly, "What book are you reading now for pleasure?" I had just finished *The Egyptian* by Mika Walteri. (I had no idea Mika was a man, however the Chairman did.) The book is a story about a physician in Egypt and my interviewer referred to the author as "him." We then talked amicably about what my life had been like, how college was going, why I wanted to be a doctor and many other things. Finally, it came time for the Chairman to leave and I walked with her to a huge, marble spiral staircase in the lobby. When she had gone up four or five steps, the chairman turned and, looking down at me, said, "I am on my way to a meeting of the Admissions Committee and I am going to recommend very highly that you be accepted here." Naturally, I was thrilled because this was her way of getting around the rules, communicating to me that I was accepted at her school and that medical school was now definitely in my future.

From this experience, I learned to keep my face on when unexpected things happened during interviews. I flew home on a plane where I sat next to a lady who proudly showed me her wrist band from her hospital stay. We were served a chicken dinner. How I was supposed to attack this meal in my crowded seat on an airplane was a mystery to me, but I really didn't care so elated was I.

The Medical School Acceptances

So there I was one spring day in college lying on my bed when there came a knock at the door. My best friend, George, now lived across the hall from me. We had an arrangement whereby if one of us went to pick up our mail he would deliver the other person's mail to his room. So, I assumed it was he and I said for him to come in. He stepped inside the door and said that he had a letter for me from the U of R medical school. I froze instantly, finally managing to croak out, "Is it thick or thin?" I should have known that my friend would do anything to create a little drama by the way he paused before he answered, but I missed that part. He finally said that it was "thick". That did the trick, releasing me from my anxiety because I knew that rejection letters were thin while acceptance letters were thick since they contained all the important documents that needed to be filled out. In truth, the letter deliverer was as thrilled as I was. Then began a day and evening of celebrating with my classmates who had been accepted at the medical school. Fifty years later nearly all of these people came back to our Class of '56 college reunion where we spent another day and evening of celebration.

An Incidental Tutor

I remember Dick for many reasons. I was best man at his wedding. In German class when I gave a perfectly inane answer to a question from the professor, he loudly announced that I had an "outstanding command of the obvious". I thought it was a marvelous comeback!

He was an outstanding scholar and helped me greatly to get through my math class. The night before the big exam, he made me memorize ten formulas for solving various problems, and instructed me just to fill in the numbers in the questions. I did just that and managed a "B" in what was otherwise a totally opaque subject to me.

The Medical School Years

Hydatidiform Mole

Before I went off to medical school, a physician friend of the family gave me a pile of medical journals (JAMA) to browse through. As school was about to begin, my roommate and I were wondering one evening whether we would be able to handle it. We felt quite confident of course, but our confidence was being eroded by our nervousness. We began to read the titles of the medical articles in the journals. The contents were on the cover so we didn't even have to open a journal. We were doing OK just trying to pronounce the words with no idea what many of them meant. Then, we got to a title about hydatidiform moles. This sent us over the edge and we spent the rest of the evening laughing and trying out different pronunciations. To this day, the mention of this word, even correctly pronounced, gets us laughing.

Iceboating

Irondequoit Bay, near the medical school, was a favorite spot to go iceboating. Boaters would lie prone on their wind-driven sailing sleds and achieve remarkable speeds over the ice. Great fun until one of the shore landowners decided that he didn't want the boaters near his property. He strung three lengths of barbed wire across the ice to keep the boaters out. An ice boater, a man of about 21 years of age, sailed right into the wires which caught him across his neck, face and scalp.

We were in a full-class session when the Chief of Plastic Surgery came to lecture. His first slide showed a red, ball-shaped arrangement of unknown, to us, identity. Urged to look closely, we all eventually spotted a tooth imbedded in the mass. Then followed a long selection of slides documenting the reconstruction of the boater's face. One hundred and twenty five long and short operations later his face looked normal with scars barely visible along his jaw lines. It took two and one-half years to complete the reconstruction which included saving about 20 of his teeth and most of the nerve functions. To think that the original injury could be repaired to the result we saw was a source of awe to all of us then and at least to me, still is today.

DVM

It was pharmacology class. We had already voted to learn how to write prescriptions in English instead of Latin. At each session we were given blank prescription pads to use in our exercises. The professor would hand our practice prescriptions back at our next session so that we could learn from our mistakes. At the bottom of each prescription was a line which ended in "MD". We all got a kick out of signing on this line. One day we were given an exercise in which the dose involved a large amount of powder. We had a chart of capsule sizes to work with. I finally managed to get all the powder into four very large capsules. Most of my classmates did the same. When we got the prescriptions back, the professor had crossed out the "MD" and written, in red, "DVM". This of course means Doctor of Veterinary Medicine and these then were prescriptions for "horse pills". None of us has ever forgotten, I'm sure, that sometimes one must use many small pills or capsules to get the whole the dose into the patient.

BCG

Since I grew up in suburban Westchester County, New York, I did not have the same exposure to diseases that someone in the middle of a big city might. So, when I got to medical school, my TB skin test was negative. It wasn't long, however, before my class was recruited into a study of the reversibility of the test. We all went to have our BCG vaccinations (protection against tuberculosis) done. Then, after some time, we were retested and lo! my TB skin test was now positive. No problem so far. When I went into the service, my test had converted back to negative. However, in the service I was exposed to a ward where active tubercular patients were treated. Not only did my TB test become positive again, but I also developed a Ghon complex (evidence of prior tuberculosis infection) in my chest which showed up sometime later in a routine chest X-ray. That was that until I began working in a clinic in the south Bronx. I was to be tested for TB about once every two years. Treatment would be instituted if I had a positive test. I was not happy about that, but my test was no longer clearly positive and so I avoided the treatment. What my TB test is now I have no idea and no one can quite follow the changes in it anyway.

Remus Roll

Anatomy lab came as a shock to most of us. The odors, the bodies and our ignorance all seemed too much to cope with. We began with the dissections as the very first class in medical school. The course was Gross Anatomy and the humor was gross, too. This story is not now acceptable—it wasn't then either but we were young and naïve. There were four people per body, but we all had to learn male and female anatomy as well. Our body was a light-skinned black man. We all named our specimens. Ours we called Remus. He was very well endowed as we say. (The genital area of the bodies were kept covered except when we were studying those organs.) A classmate and I went to a small store near our apartment where they were selling breads and pastries. On a top shelf there were long rolls. My classmate, a wag to begin with, announced to the clerk that he would like a Remus roll. That about finished me for the day. Even now, though we no longer think that this was funny, the two of us chuckle when reminded of the story.

Alopecia Totalis

One of my closest friends in college, the aforementioned tutor, Dick, and I would often go to his family's house in Batavia, NY for the weekend. His mom and dad were wonderful people and very good to me. His mother had the most beautiful auburn hair imaginable which people often commented on. After college, he went his way and I went to medical school nearby.

One day while roaming around the medical wards I came upon his mother standing just outside her room. She was wearing a kerchief-cum-turban around her head. We had a pleasant conversation—I did not know why she was in the hospital—and I continued on my way wondering what had become of her lovely hair. Later, Dick told me that she did not have any hair at all (alopecia totalis) but that she owned two very expensive wigs. While one was out being cleaned and cared for, she would wear the other. Very few people look as well in their own hair as this lady did in her wig!

A Christian Scientist

One of my best friends in medical school was a chemical engineer by training since his father refused to pay for any other education for him. Hence, he was forced to pay for medical school himself. Tom was a musician, a largely self taught virtuoso at the organ and a terrific piano player as well. He auditioned for the job of organist at the First Church of Christ Scientist in Rochester among sharp competition given that the Eastman School of Music, like the medical school, was a part of the University. He was hired immediately and began playing for services at the church. There was much sought after vocal talent in town for the churches, and one "diva" sang at the Christian Scientist Church. Tom however, made a serious error by leaving several of his medical school books under the organ where they were eventually discovered. His contact telephone number was, of all places, the Anatomy Department. The call telling him he had been fired came to him there. The following Sunday, a new person sat at the organ in church. The vocalist got up to sing, noted that Tom was not at the organ and said, "I do not sing without Mr. Harter!" Then she sat down. The following Sunday, he was back playing the organ having promised to never ever do anything that would connect him with the medical school. And he was able to continue to finance his education.

The Bakery Truck

It was the middle of winter in Rochester, NY. My roommate and I lived in an apartment in the low-rent district. We were first year medical students. It had snowed all night and was terribly cold, below zero, and very windy. My car, parked behind the apartment, would not start and was buried in snow as well.

So we set out, bundled up, to the main road early in the morning. Of course, everything had been plowed already, Rochester being set up to deal with snow. We were looking for a ride and, sure enough, along came a bakery truck. The driver stopped for us and said that he was going up toward the University but would have to drop us off on the far side of the bridge over the Genesee River so as to keep to his schedule.

Off we went, warm in the truck for a 3-4 mile ride to a place in sight of the medical school on the other side of the Genesee River. Well, I have been cold before and since but never as badly as while we were crossing that bridge in howling wind and a deep freeze. That evening, having been delivered home by a classmate, we dug my car out, got it running and were good to go for the next day. Winter in Rochester is only a minor inconvenience but my roommate and I will ever be thankful for the bakery truck driver's help.

Right Hand Turns

In my second year of college I acquired a car, the mouse-brown limousine previously mentioned. In my first year of medical school, my car had a run-in with some metal warning signs placed in the middle of Main Street. I knew that the left front fender was bent, but I didn't realize the consequences of that until the next morning. After the accident, I turned right a couple of times onto my street and into my driveway. The next morning we realized that turning left was impossible with the damage done. This posed a problem as we set out for school. It took a long time to get there devising a route as we went along which enabled us to end up in the school parking lot having executed right turns only. Somehow we made it, probably by making a very wide left turn somewhere along the way. Bending the fender back toward normal with a crowbar permanently solved the problem so that I could round corners again in any direction.

Bacteriology

At one point in my high school study of physics I was doing poorly. My father and my physics teacher were very close friends and colleagues. From my desk in the front row I could hardly fail to see my father come into the room and immediately disappear into Mr. Wilson's lab. I knew there was trouble afoot. At dinner that night, my father said, "You are not distinguishing yourself in physics." No reply was forthcoming from me and my father never said another word about it. Since the time to take the New York State Regents exams was nearing, I studied a bit harder and thankfully passed the physics exam with a fairly presentable B grade. That was good enough to get into college.

Many years later I was having trouble with a subject in the medical school curriculum. This time it was bacteriology/parasitology. The department chairman called me into his office essentially to put me on notice. During the interview he went to his files and brought out my folder. He said, after looking it over, "You are not distinguishing yourself in bacteriology." Déjà vu. This time I was able to croak out a question, "Am I still in medical school?" It seemed that I was but that depended on how well I did on the upcoming parasitology exam. Once again, I studied a bit more, eventually scoring in the high eighties on the National Board Examination in Bacteriology, taken at the end of the second year of medical school. Saved by the book!

I took parasitology the semester I got married and I didn't much like the course. It seemed that I was always too busy to study the course material. Eventually, as it was important for me to do so, I passed the course. During the following summer while I was working in the bacteriology lab on a fellowship grant examining the role of phage viruses, professors, instructors and students all ate lunch together. The professors were not much older than the rest of us. We would have lively discussions of politics, religion, etc. Never one to keep my mouth judiciously closed, I once stated an opinion of mine in direct opposition to that of the parasitology professor. He looked at me and said, "Remember, Hermance, your grade is still in pencil." That was enough to settle the argument in his favor.

Pass the Pipette

The summer before my junior year in med school, I worked for my bacteriology professor on a March of Dimes grant. He was doing research on phage viruses. My job in the lab was to do the busy work. I would use a glass pipette, suck the serum containing the virus (phage) to a measured point in the pipette and then deposit that onto an agar covered glass Petri dish. I was surrounded by glass tubes and Petri dishes. This was such a

repetitive job (during which I only occasionally pipetted some material into my mouth) that I dreamed about it. One night I actually asked my wife while I was asleep to "pass the pipette"! She thought that was hysterically funny. I thought it less so but the story brings back memories of a very satisfactory time in my life.

Indian Curry

The same professor and his wife threw a dinner party for the department one evening. His wife was from India and she had just received a shipment of Indian foods and spices. The table was laden with delicious looking foods, some of which looked as if they might be very hot and spicy. My exposure to this cuisine was minimal up to then. Before long I was in need of something to counteract the hot spices in the food I was eating and I spied a small dish of what looked like pineapple preserve. Just the ticket I thought and I put some on my plate and ate a small forkful. Well, I thought I would burst into flames! I had never before experienced anything so hot. I couldn't just spit it out so I swallowed it and then had to dab my eyes which were tearing heavily by then. All this transpired without anyone noticing except my wife who kept still until she found what the outcome of my discomfort would be. Eventually, with enough water—I knew it was water—and some other non-spicy items, I recovered. Ever since however, I have been very careful when sampling unknown foods especially garnishes and side dishes as when my present employer, also from India, takes me out to the Indian restaurant for lunch. He is always very good about pointing out the "safe" foods.

Statistics

Sometime during my junior year in medical school, the class was informed that a statistics class was going to become part of the curriculum and would be mandatory. Calculus had not been a requirement for medical school in those days as it is now. I doubt that some of us, including me, would have become doctors. No prior discussion except to express our horror took place among my classmates to my knowledge. However, no one showed up for the class when it was first scheduled and not for the second scheduled time either. The idea of a statistics class died a quiet death. Naturally, I had classmates who were already good at statistics and we all had to learn some of the subject as we continued our studies, so important are statistics in the medical literature.

Psychiatric Interviewing

In Wing R, as the psychiatric building was called, was a classroom with a one-way glass wall. Here, the part of the class rotating through Psychiatry would sit while a classmate interviewed a real patient. Afterward, the class and the professor would critique the session. Of course, criticism by one's peers is often more anxiety provoking than that of the professor, but not being able to see the class was of some help. While I don't remember the content of my interview, I do remember the class discussion afterward. I did fairly well as did most of us, having been trained extensively in history taking (the most important part of any medical exam). One fault about my technique did come up which I never forgot and about which I would often think in my medical career. It seemed that I tended to put a little more physical space between me and the patient than was necessary, perhaps leading to a feeling of aloofness or, worse, disinterest on my part. Not what I intended nor the way I felt, but still in need of correction.

One of the teaching exercises we were assigned in psychiatry was to follow certain patients and to interview their families. There didn't seem to be too much trouble getting the family of my patient together so we all met one evening in a small conference room. (If one did not have prior experience conducting a meeting this was a fast way to learn for sure.) I was amazed at the insights the family members had into their relative's troubles. Nowadays of course, medications would probably have kept him out of the hospital, but that course was not open to us then. So, we spent an hour discussing what the patient's problem was, how he got that way, what family members could do about it and what his care would consist of once he was discharged. It's hard to imagine that they were impressed with me, but I surely was impressed by them and I think they went away feeling that the good of their relative was uppermost in the minds of his hospital caregivers.

Another less inspiring incident took place during my psychiatry rotation. Each private room in Wing R had a light next to the door. If it was red it meant that the patient was not to be disturbed. I knew this, but whether the light was on by my patient's door or I just didn't notice I cannot say. One afternoon however, I breezed into this female patient's room with my clipboard intent on interviewing her. The room lights were off as I settled near the head of her bed and was just about to proceed when I realized that something was not quite right. Indeed, there were two people in her bed, both momentarily lying quite still. It was the patient and her husband I came to find out. I don't remember if I said anything as I made my escape, embarrassment being uppermost in my mind.

The Sigmoidoscopy

When I was rotating through medicine I went to watch a sigmoidoscopy with some classmates. The patient was a woman and the instructor was early in his residency. We were there to observe the technique and no one expected abnormal findings. Just after the procedure began the resident noted an "annular lesion" which we all took turns observing. This was a doughnut-shaped lesion which we all knew was potentially a very serious problem. Of course, a biopsy was taken, further enhancing our training that day. A few days later, the pathology report was returned. The diagnosis? Normal cervix. And so, we learned even more, namely to make sure that the orifice through which an exam is being conducted is the correct one.

Antidiuretic Hormone

One afternoon the class assembled in the main lecture hall per schedule. Earlier in the day I had had a shot, planned, of antidiuretic hormone, but later it never occurred to me to sit somewhere near an exit at our afternoon meeting. So I took my customary place in the middle of the seats. About 15 minutes into the lecture it became obvious that the hormone had worn off. I jumped up, made my way out of the row and out of the lecture hall as fast as I could to the great amusement of my classmates. Even I thought it was funny and we all learned much about antiduretics and how they work that day.

Cloudy Serum

From time to time in medical school it became necessary for us to collect blood samples from each other for later study. One such effort took place when we were juniors and subject to "Third Year Disease", an affliction in which one thinks one has all the diseases that one has ever studied—or at least the worst ones. After we had drawn blood from one another, the samples were carefully labeled with our names and placed in the walk-in refrigerator for storage. One of my classmates had occasion to go into the refrigerator while the tubes were still there. He casually looked through the rows of tubes and noticed that there was one tube in which the serum was white rather than a clear golden color, the blood cells having settled out during storage. He pulled that tube out of the rack to have a better look and discovered it had his name on it. That was all he needed to see—soon the entire class knew that he had a very serious medical condition. Of course, he didn't have anything wrong, his finding being a normal variant, quite common and not at all indicative of disease. For a while though, Dwight had a very bad case of Third Year Disease.

Vitamin B12

My dear friend George called me one day after I had started medical school. He had been to see his physician who prescribed a Vitamin B12 shot for sciatica (it worked, I know not why). Would I be able to administer the injection he asked. He would be my orange he said, knowing that we sometimes practiced giving injections on oranges. He came to my garret apartment to have the deed done. Well, how would he know that I had not yet administered an injection to any one? Also, no one had yet told me how painful a Vitamin B12 shot could be. The directions said to administer the injection in the buttock, so that is what I did. I must say that George was very good about not fainting dead away but he knew that something had gone on behind him. His first comment after recovering a bit was, "I'll bet that was the first shot you ever gave wasn't it?" I admitted it, George recovered and we remained best friends.

"I'm Having My baby!"

Early in my junior year of medical school, everyone in the class was assigned to follow a newly pregnant woman upon her arrival at the obstetrics clinic. This assignment took precedent over our other activities—we were to be on call to attend her at all times and could be called out of whatever class activities we were engaged in whenever she arrived at the hospital. Naturally, we got to know our ladies very well while we were learning how to properly follow a pregnancy. I knew my patient had had several normal pregnancies. When my patient was near term, I was called because she was in labor and already in a labor room. When I arrived, she said that she had come by taxi to the hospital and had had just two labor pains. (We were to call them "contractions" not pains.) Surely, she was not very far along in labor. I examined her and left to stand just outside the room in case she needed me. I awaited the resident in charge. As I was talking with a passing classmate, I heard my patient call from the labor room, "Doctor, I'm havin' my baby!" Indeed she was and I proceeded to deliver a fine baby boy. Paying attention only to what I was doing, I tied and cut the umbilical cord and prepared to show a very vocal infant to his mother. When I looked up there stood a bevy of nursing students with their instructor and my resident. The nurses had been passing by and stopped to observe the proceedings. Not until then did I feel even a little nervous. The baby was whisked off to the nursery to be weighed and evaluated. And then I began to feel quite proud of myself. (I still do over this event at least.) Later, the mother said that she had had three contractions, one at home, one in the taxi and the final one in the labor room. This was an excellent lesson in taking a complete history. Later also, the OB-GYN section had a serious discussion at higher levels about how to avoid a similar situation in the future, but I didn't get in any trouble at all as my classmates confidently predicted I would. Thankfully, my training up until then had been quite thorough and all I really did were things I had seen done before.

A Ruined Coat

One evening in the midst of winter in Rochester, I was hanging out in the OB section of the hospital with no specific assignment to perform. Suddenly, the doors to the anteroom of the delivery room flew open and a lady in labor arrived. Her fur coat, which she was still wearing, was trailing off the back of the gurney. I stood there and watched a very quick delivery. As the baby was rushed off to the delivery room, the new mother turned to me and said, "Damn, I've ruined my coat!" I looked closely to see what damage may have been done and then assured her that her coat was undamaged. "Great," she said, "What'd I have?" She had had a healthy baby boy and was quite happy about that outcome, too.

Mr. Smith

While rotating through the surgery service, we spent several weeks in urology. We were not on the service all day every day but we did make morning rounds with the attending doctors. There were about half a dozen of us doing this and we were assigned patients in rotation as they were admitted to the hospital. My first patient was a Mr. Smith. I completed his workup and presented his case one morning. Quite by chance, my next patient was named Smith. That, of course, caused amusement among my classmates, but they were positively hysterical when my third urology patient was Mr. Smith, too. Just a wee bit suspicious, I checked the rotation list to find that he had been assigned to me out of turn by the resident who didn't want to interfere with a good thing. I managed to keep all these Smiths straight, but the favorite question to me each day was, naturally, "How is Mr. Smith doing?"

Legs

Unused as I was to having my legs admired, I was most interested in a classmate's remark as we were waiting in our skivvies to go into the "hot" room while involuntarily participating in another experiment, this one in physiology. Said he, "You look like you must have been a football player." Touch football once in a while as a kid but none after that I hastened to inform him. Then we went into the "hot" room to sweat, whirl thermometers around and undertake other interesting activities in the name of science. I have no idea what prompted his remark, but I do have big legs.

Birds, for the

One of my classmates who went on to become a very famous physician-administrator in New York City was married to the daughter of the author of the most widely used pediatric textbook, then and now. She and her sister were hired to do the extensive index to the first edition. It must truly have been a massive job. One understands why the sisters would have been happy to complete it. I'm not sure when they added the entry, but there in the "B" section of the index was the listing, "Birds, for the, pages 1-1413". I saw it for myself! I'm told their father was not happy but surely he had to be amused. Future editions do not have that reference.

Gypsies

In the southern tier of New York State, south of Rochester, there were and may still be gypsy campgrounds. A gypsy chief arrived at the hospital one day requesting to see a surgeon. It seems there was a sick person in the encampment who needed to have a doctor visit. One of the staff went with the chief to the encampment where he found a young man lying outside of the main tent. The doctor was asked to examine the man, which he did. He announced that there was nothing wrong with the man except that his heart was on the right side of his chest, usually a normal variant. With that, the doctor was escorted into the tent where the truly ill patient lay. The doctor arranged for the patient to be sent to the hospital, now with the approval of the gypsies.

For several days after this event, there were gypsies all over the hospital, but there was never any trouble with them so far as I knew. Eventually, the patient recovered, the visitors were happy and the attending physician was congratulated for his astuteness.

Ardmore Street

After I got married we lived in an apartment in a converted house on Ardmore Street in Rochester. This was not the high rent district. Among my classmates there was an annual competition to see who paid the least rent for their apartments. Peggy and I won each year. But, one day while

Peggy was pregnant, the landlord raised our rent. It went from $60.00 per month to $65.00. So, we paid our landlord a visit in his Rochester business office. He was quite pleasant, possibly because of Peggy's condition and the fact that I was a starving medical student. At any rate, we came to an agreement; I would mow the not very big lawn and shovel the snow off of the short front walk and he would not raise the rent.

A Different Competition

There was another competition in our class, as well. One of my classmate's wives was pregnant. What was unusual was that her mother was also pregnant, due around the same time as her daughter. We were amused by the stories my classmate's wife told about the ways in which her mother was in competition with her. Near term for both of them, her mother was in a serious automobile crash. Fortunately both expectant mother and her child survived. My classmate's wife readily agreed that her mother had won the competition and that she was glad to have that part of her pregnancy over with. We were able to laugh at all this because no tragedy came to either the new or the older mother.

Grass

Just after we moved into our garret apartment we had two snowstorms about a week apart each about three feet deep. It was an exceptionally snowy winter even for Rochester. On a day in April while my wife was looking out the window, she said, "Do you have sidewalks here?" I replied that of course we had sidewalks. Then she said, "I know you don't have grass!" Luckily the next two winters were not as bad, but unfortunately, given our rental agreement, the grass did reappear each year.

Wann Lassen Sie den andere Schuh Fallen?

There is an old German story about a man who always dropped his first shoe noisily and his other shoe quietly. To listeners this may have given rise to the phrase "waiting for the other shoe to fall". As newlyweds, our bedroom had one small area of wall behind which was our neighbors' bedroom closet. Herb and Charlotte, an older couple who eventually became good friends of ours, lived next door. Shortly after our arrival while we were in bed we heard Herb drop his shoe in his closet. However, we never did hear the other one hit the floor. Since it was clear that Herb could plainly hear everything that went on in our bedroom from inside his closet, we decided that he did not want us to know that he was in there. This sent us into gales of laughter and we actually did hear a chuckle from the other side of the partition. When I think of it, I wonder that Peggy and I never gave Herb's eaves-dropping another thought. Now, however as we look back, we are still waiting to hear the other shoe drop and still laughing about our apartment on Ardmore Street.

We were friendly with our downstairs neighbors, too. Peggy saw them preparing to leave in a taxi and found out then that they were on their way to a famous hospital in Boston. The wife had a serious medical problem and they were going to have it treated. Less than 48 hours they returned. It seems that when the house officer at the Boston hospital came to admit our neighbor, he was astonished to find that they had come from Rochester. He could not understand why they were in Boston instead of at Strong Memorial Hospital in Rochester. He indicated that there wasn't anything that could be done there that couldn't be done in Rochester, and so back they came. I remember that our neighbor recovered after being admitted to Strong. I often wonder why patients go from one place with an excellent medical center to another one far away, unless there is clearly no place nearby which could handle the medical problem.

The Halloween Party

George came for supper on Halloween, 1959. Earlier that day Peggy and I drove over a wide, bumpy set of railroad tracks in town. My wife was very pregnant and anxious to get things moving. She managed to produce supper which included peaches in syrup for dessert. Just as I was about to have some, she announced that she thought she might be going into labor. Had the railroad track trip worked? I spilled peaches down the front of my shirt.

George said that he would drive behind us to the hospital since he was never very confident that my car would get us where we wanted to go. So, off we went, Peggy complaining that she guessed that she would miss our class Halloween costume party. She was admitted promptly, her doctor, the chief resident in OB-GYN was there and, once she was settled in, I left for the party in a room five stories below. Then I began going up and down (thank God for Mr. Otis) keeping a check on things. Between the peaches and eventually having been thrown up on it probably seemed as if I was in a costume, too. (On one of my visits to Peggy, she beckoned to me from the labor room doorway to come over to her in bed. I did, whereupon she threw up on me.)

Her labor continued and the party broke up. It looked as if we were not going to have a Halloween baby. When Peggy was taken into the delivery room, I stayed out at the desk. Several people called to see how things were coming along. About 1:00 AM, November 1, Peggy delivered our son weighing 9 pounds, 11 ounces and perfectly healthy. I called a buddy of mine, a classmate who, I knew would still be up, with the news, checked on my wife and son and went home to wash up. Eventually, I went to George's apartment where we ate toast and blueberry jam and I tried to relax.

In those days, new mothers and babies were kept in the hospital for a few days, five in Peggy's case, so, between my hospital duties and visiting my wife and son, I rarely went home. Since it was November in Rochester we had lots of snow by the time Billy and Peggy came home and we were able to start to adjust to a whole new life.

Shut up, Hilara

My mother, Hilara, came to help out with the new baby. She was stunned that we carried on around the baby in our usual way, talking, not whispering, walking around, not tiptoeing, having some music playing, fixing meals with the usual noise. This was not what she had done with her only child.

My father, George, arrived a few days later while Billy was having a nap. He tiptoed into the bedroom, whispering all the time, to see his new grandson. My mother said quite authoritatively, "It's perfectly all right to make all the noise you want around the baby, George." He looked over his shoulder and replied, "Shut up, Hilara." This caused Peggy and me to burst out laughing because we knew that this would happen. As old school as they were about babies, they both eventually came around to being at ease with Billy. My father soon thought nothing of lifting him out of his crib so that Billy could continue his naps on his grandpa's chest. Billy became his "Honey-man" since one could not possibly call a boy simply "Honey".

A $25.00 Check

From the time I started college up until I got married, my father sent $25.00 each week for my living expenses. While he loved Peggy, he was not happy that we had gotten married while I was still in medical school. For some reason, he continued to pay for my books. But there were no more $25.00 checks, or tuition payments for that matter. Not too bad while Peggy was working, but we eventually did have to have a loan to finish school. About one week after Billy was born there arrived in the mail a check from my father for $25.00 and the checks continued every week until I graduated. The man was not about to be blamed for anything that Billy might lack. He never mentioned the checks to me and I never mentioned them to him. They did make life a bit easier for us.

A Big Baby

There were several new babies in our class. Billy was by far the biggest one. When the dean's wife threw her annual lawn party, someone put an empty beer can in Billy's hands to the amusement of the guests. I'm not sure his mother was amused, but she understood the joke!

Rabbi Hyman

My cousin Henry Hyman was chronically ill for several years. He would frequently find himself in Strong Memorial Hospital. One day a stranger appeared in his room and announced that he had come to see who the other Henry Hyman was. The stranger turned out to be a Rabbi and my cousin and he had a light-hearted conversation about the coincidence of their names.

The Aorta

Once again I am in the emergency room but this time I am still in medical school. I was in my junior year and I was actually on my way home after a day on the wards when I was, for all intents and purposes, snatched up and deposited in the main ER operating room. With only a little time to scrub, I was helped into a gown and gloved and masked. There were three others at the table, two residents and an attending surgeon. I was told to stand next to the attending and that I was in charge of "proximal control". What this might be I had no idea. When I looked about I was now surrounded by tables full of sterile equipment. I was thoroughly trapped! The patient, by now already anesthetized had just arrived in the ER with a rupturing aorta. Even I knew this was not good.

Thankfully, the surgeon explained what I was to do when proximal control was necessary. At some point during the next few hours in order for me to perform "distal control" it became necessary for me to move to the other side of the surgeon. One of the nurses was ready to correct my turn so as to have the front of me always facing the sterile fields surrounding me. Many hours later the surgery was completed, the patient doing very well (he survived to continue his life with an aortic prosthesis in place) and I was preparing to leave. A resident suggested that I do a blood volume study on the patient before I left. Since I had never done such a thing and since I was half dead by now, I simply refused and left.

Thinking that I would no longer be attending medical school for being insubordinate, I went home and went to sleep. In the morning, I got ready to take a bath—our apartment lacked a shower—and as I did so I put my hand into the water to test its temperature. I let out a yelp, not because the water was too hot but because all of my fingertips were painful and burning which was made worse by the heat of the water. It took a while for it to dawn on me that there had been little vacuums in the finger tips of my sterile gloves and that blood had pooled in the tips of my fingers making them excruciatingly sensitive. During the day the sensation wore off, I wasn't dismissed from my medical studies and I decided that surgery was not for me.

Vaginal Bleeding

Once again I was in the ER at night, trying to get a little sleep when I was called out to see a young woman with vaginal bleeding. I examined her as thoroughly as I knew how and didn't find anything wrong with the lady. The on-call attending was a woman who graciously came to the hospital to see the patient. With me at her side, she did another pelvic and abdominal exam and asked a few questions. The patient, it turned out, had had her first baby at about age 13 before her first menstrual bleeding occurred and had nursed all of her babies. This then, was her first normal menstrual period! Another excellent lesson for me about how essential a good medical history is.

The Glasses

It used to bother me when my wife and I were dating that she rarely wore her glasses. At the movies, for example, she would put them on but soon would put them back in her pocketbook. I finally gave up trying to get her to use them until after we were married when I suggested that she have her eyes checked in ophthalmology. The chief of the department did her exam. Now, her parents had spent a fair amount of money on Peggy's glasses when money was not in abundance. The doctor asked her after his exam if she had her glasses with her. When she produced them, the doctor took them and tossed them in the waste basket! It turned out, of course, that she had not needed glasses in the first place. When informed of this finding, I did not say, "I told you so", and, to her credit, Peggy did not use this line on me either.

Discrimination?

For many years, perhaps from its inception, my medical school had classes of about 70 students. Almost every class I am told, including mine, had two female students and one minority student. Eventually, I guess, the State of New York took a look at this arrangement and decided that a more equitable setup should prevail. For all I know, there might have been financial consequences if changes were not made. Today, each class has about 50% women and many minority and foreign students. And, I have always been amused by the fact that the top two students in my class were the two ladies, who, I am sure, turned out to be terrific doctors.

Some Dear Friends

In the years since college my wife and I have spent many happy hours with the Powells.

Bill is a college and medical school classmate of mine and Peggy and Sally are good friends. Since we had no money, entertainment consisted of playing bridge at someone's house and sipping wine coolers (cheap). First we had to learn how to play bridge however, so the Powells and my wife and I taught ourselves. Hilarious! Then, we would get together with others and we would all have our babies with us. There was constant jumping up and down from the tables to see to it that the babies were not too warm or too cold This was accompanied by opening and closing the bedroom window, each mother having a different idea of the ideal temperature. What fun we had.

Then there was the trip to the wine country south of Rochester in the Finger Lakes Region. Though each winery had strict limits on samples we would manage to get a slight buzz on for free while winery hopping.

And there was a wonderful trip to Nantucket with the Powells. We rode bikes, visited the lighthouses, ate as inexpensively as we could. We stayed in one room in a motel. This required one or the other couple to take an occasional nocturnal stroll. When it came time to go home to Rochester, we discovered that we had enough money among us to get off the Island and to buy gas but not to buy food. So, we found a UofR alumnus who agreed to have the four of us to dinner, and then we went on our way. On the ride home with Sally asleep in the back seat we stopped to spend the last of our change on ice cream cones. Sally woke up while we were driving along having our treats and was quite put out. To this day she still bristles when reminded of our nighttime treachery.

After one trip which we took in Bill's car because of the sad condition of mine, my car broke down between the Powells' place and ours. It was 4:00

AM and Peggy was pregnant. Luckily it was summertime. There we were right in front of Wuzzy's Bar and Grill. (I kid you not.) So I called Bill to relate our plight and to solicit help. Since he thought it was a joke, I had to put Wuzzy himself on the phone interrupting his cleaning up duties. Even then Bill didn't believe me but came to rescue us just in case, looking out for Peggy most likely. Another story that causes much amusement when we get together now.

Cows and Horses

The Powells had a pretty little daughter, Suzie. Our children went everywhere with us because babysitters cost money. In those days we would drive to see our friends or relatives. We passed many farm animals on these trips and for some perverse reason I thought it would be fun to teach Suzie that cows were horses and vice versa. It was easy to do and no one seemed to object until it became obvious that Suzie did actually have them mixed up. Eventually of course she found out which was which. We have kept up with Suzie, her family and career over the years and whenever we are together the cows and horses story comes up, to the befuddlement of Suzie's husband. Didn't seem to harm her development at all since she has a highly successful career and lovely family.

Penzoil

Sally Powell is a stunning redhead. After graduation, Bill and Sally decamped for Cleveland. We kept in close touch and visited as often as we could, as we still do. One day, I was thumbing through an issue of Look Magazine when, to my amazement, I came across a full page picture of Sally in a Penzoil ad. It turned out that Sally had gone to an agency in Cleveland with the idea of seeing if she could get some modeling work. She had absolutely no training or experience for this in her background. She instantly landed the Penzoil assignment. Bill was not happy and indicated that it would be best if Sally stayed home and tended to the kids. As far as I know, that was the beginning and the end of a promising career.

Some Vegetation

Four couples met for dinner one night. Three couples knew Peggy and me but did not know one another. It fell to me to introduce the Roots to the Weeds and the Branches. A real ice-breaker.

Thirty-two Girls

A medical student I knew about in school was a sperm donor. He eventually got married and had three children, all girls. Wondering whether he and his wife should try once more for a boy, he went to the professor who had been in charge of the sperm bank hoping to find out if he was able to sire males. Of course, he had signed papers of confidentiality so the professor was not happy about this request for information But, I suppose the professor was curious, too, so he did look up the man's records. Our donor had had thirty-two girls. That was the end of his hopes for a boy.

Hunderful Wunny

The period leading up to the Intern Matching Program results was a stressful one. I knew where I wanted to do my internship and, contrary to the rules, I had been given a fairly good idea that I would be accepted there. (Getting to the interview at Ninth Avenue and 59th Street in Manhattan had been daunting in itself, made worse by several unsuccessful attempts to cross Ninth Avenue without getting killed.) I was treated with the utmost consideration and was impressed with the committee members, all senior attendings, the paneled conference room and especially with the resident assigned to escort me around the hospital. His best moment came when he showed me the bullet hole in the screen door of the emergency room. The Roosevelt Hospital it seemed was in a very rough neighborhood.

Eventually the assignment results arrived on intern matching day and I had obtained a position at Roosevelt. I called my wife at home immediately. So excited was she that she exclaimed, "Hunderful wunny, hunderful wunny!" I knew what she meant and that she shared my excitement. I spent four years at The Roosevelt Hospital and then joined the attending staff. It was a very exciting and rewarding time of my life.

No Parking Card, No Degree

In order to park at Strong Memorial Hospital one needed a card to gain entrance to the lot. We did not receive our actual diplomas at the graduation ceremony, but were instructed to pick them up at the Registrar's Office. We were all packed and ready to leave when I went to get my diploma. There, I was informed that I could not pickup my parchment until I had turned in my parking card which I knew was already packed in a suitcase somewhere. So I would have to send that back and have my degree mailed to me. My father's comment on all this was, "I wish I had known that all you needed was a parking card to get your MD degree." I think he had the money he had spent in mind.

The Post-Graduate
Training Years

The Emergency Room

The Emergency Room was to me by far the most exciting place to work in the hospital. One never knew when certain skills would be needed. Indeed, many ways of doing things would be invented (or reinvented) on the spot. The main drawback to emergency medicine in my view was the lack of follow-up with the patients. They would be treated and discharged, never to be seen again or disappear into the hospital for further treatment. Rarely was there time to check on a patient later, but I would sometimes hear what his or her ultimate fate had been.

Of course, there was one advantage; when quitting time came one could leave the problems of the day behind while unfinished cases would become someone else's problem. Usually, but not always!

Under The Sink

Many were the men and women who arrived in the ER in a state of inebriation. Often, they were brought in by the police, sometimes so drunk as to be semiconscious. However, one never knew—other problems such as diabetic complications could mimic drunkenness. So it was important that all of these individuals be thoroughly examined and properly diagnosed, even the ones who were regulars. There was not room in the ER to place these people in beds and even then it would have been unsafe to do so. Therefore, a place was set aside under the sink in the largest utility room where the patient, on a cushion, would not injure himself and could be observed frequently.

Naturally, after leaving the ER after a hard day's work one did not expect to encounter the same patients the next day. One afternoon and evening I had had an especially difficult time with a woman who was intoxicated. She was eventually placed "under the sink". As I left to go home I must have expressed my exasperation with this patient to the people coming on shift.

When I arrived for my shift the next morning I was greeted by several of my "colleagues" who were standing by the wheelchair in which they had placed my by now very hung over patient. Thus, I would have to deal with the lady for several more hours. They thought that this was very funny and eagerly awaited my reaction. They were not disappointed since now I was even more exasperated with them than with the patient. My friend eventually was able to leave the ER and thankfully did not return that evening!

If I Am Found Dead . . .

Behind the staff doing their paperwork in the original Roosevelt Hospital Emergency Room was a large plate glass window overlooking a fairly large waiting room. On my first day as a resident in medicine assigned to the ER, while I was finishing up a chart, I noticed a commotion in the waiting room. It revolved around a woman who seemed to be having a sudden problem of some sort. She was taken into the nearest room, the minor OR, and settled on the table there. The nurse in charge directed me, specifically, to attend to the patient. I did a thorough exam after listening to her complaints and then went over things again because I could not find evidence of a medical problem. I assumed that was because of lack of experience on my part. I reported my lack of findings to the head nurse. We agreed that the patient should remain in the waiting room for a time so that she could be observed. Shortly thereafter as I checked through the glass window I saw that the woman was writing on a long slip of paper which, I later found out, she kept in her bra instead of her pocketbook. What was she doing I inquired of the nurse. Barely able to contain herself, the nurse explained that the patient recognized me as new to the ER and she had gone into her usual act when she spotted a new doctor. She was adding me to the list of all the medical personnel including nurses who had also not found anything wrong with her. It was labeled, "If I am found dead, the following people killed me." The first name on the list was the very same nurse I was working with that evening who had worked in the ER for many years. Over the next few years, I got to know this "patient" quite well. She often said her rosary in the waiting room and we would sometimes walk together to services in the church across the street. I also saw her often seated at her card table on the streets around the church selling chances for various church fund-raisers. We never discussed her list.

St. Patrick's Day

The busiest day and night of the year in our Emergency Room was, without question, St. Patrick's Day. The alcohol problems were legion, but the trouble resulting from brawls was more serious. It was possible to slip on the blood in the hallway, often mixed with rain water and melting snow. There was suturing going on non-stop and occasionally people would have to be prepared for the operating rooms upstairs. Needless to say, the "under the sink" crowd was large and it was a busy/hectic scene.

The Egg

When I was an intern we were allowed to watch and help out in the step-down area next to the ER. One evening while I was there a man and woman were sent to the area to have a very delicate procedure done. It seems that during sex play the woman had inserted an uncooked egg straight from the refrigerator into her partner's rectum (I am not making this up!)

The egg got stuck, still intact, which accounted, I suppose, for the odd gait that the man had upon arrival in the ER. Naturally, the egg had to be removed and so I learned a technique which luckily I never had to use. A very careful administration of a dose of olive oil was delivered into the rectum in question and then the egg was punctured, the contents of the egg spilled out and the egg collapsed. The oil prevented any injury to the surrounding tissues as the egg shell broke apart and was expelled. At the time I thought that this was the cleverest thing I had ever seen and, of course, the whole idea was terribly funny to me as well. The patient quickly recovered his dignity and left. I hope he never tried this again. If he had used a hard-boiled egg, extraction of the foreign body would have been more difficult.

The Non-Alcoholic

In the same area where the egg episode took place some people spent days while the hospital operated at 100% capacity. My job one day was to take an admission history and perform an admission physical exam. I introduced myself to a very distinguished looking middle-aged man whose excellent color did not immediately suggest illness. His admitting diagnosis however was cirrhosis of the liver. The reason this man stands out in my memory is apparent from his history. He was an executive high up in the railroad industry and, I gathered, did most of his work at lunch and dinner with other businessmen. He actually admitted to having a fair amount of alcohol to drink as a normal part of his day but did not consider himself to be an alcoholic. Lunch always began with several drinks. During most afternoons there would be more drinks in business offices and boardrooms. He dined out virtually every night on business with several drinks, wine and after-dinner drinks. He rode in the bar car on his commute to the suburbs, and there was always a nightcap at home. Heaven knows what happened on weekends! However, as part of his talk with me he noted that he had never been drunk and that no one had ever seen him function below top notch because of alcohol. It occurred to me that there was always a minimum level of alcohol in his blood stream, and that his liver was ruined having to continuously process the chemical. In reality, no one knew what he was like without his alcohol dose. He eventually died in the hospital from bleeding esophageal varices, a direct result of his liver disease.

The Wrong Way Ride

Whenever the police found a new physician in the ER, they would zero in on him (not usually her) in order I suppose to have a little fun. One evening I was called to go in the patrol car to an intersection nearby because of a report of a man lying in the street. I knew the location was north of the hospital but was alarmed and then really frightened to find that, indeed, we were going north, on Ninth Avenue which is one-way going south! It was a fast ride during which I rode with my feet on the dashboard. Then, to get to the scene we drove west on an east-bound street. When we got there, the "patient" had gotten up and wandered off, but many people had witnessed this so there really had been the potential for trouble. Ever after, as I got to know New York City's Finest, I was reminded of this ride and my reaction to it. Everyone except me thought it was hilarious, but I was just happy to have lived through it unscathed.

Illegal Turn

Getting to know the police did have benefits, however. About three years after the story above, I turned off of the West Side Highway at 72nd Street because the traffic ahead of me on the Highway was at a standstill. It was the end of another busy day for me. I was still wearing my hospital whites and driving my little red Volkswagen. I knew all the reasonable routes around traffic jams on my way to and from work. At the stoplight, I made a left onto Riverside Drive to continue my trip north. I was immediately pulled over for making this (unknown to me) illegal turn. About half-way through his review of my "error" the officer stopped, peered closely at me and began to chuckle. He had identified me as the "Doc" known for his one-way rides. Then he bawled me out, but he didn't give me a ticket and we had a friendly little chat before I went on my way. Never again did I make that wrong turn and, over the years, I have often thought of this brush with the law.

No MD License Plates

In January, 1962, while I was still working in the ER, a monumental snowstorm swept down upon New York City. I remember especially how quiet the area around the hospital became for several days. There was so much snow that the City actually closed. No unnecessary vehicles were to be allowed into Manhattan. And, I had to get to the hospital! However, I did not yet have my New York State License and therefore I did not have

MD plates (my father always maintained that MD stood for "muddled driver"). I would be wearing my hospital whites driving into the City but I did not have a good way of proving that I actually was a doctor. Finally, I took my framed medical diploma off the wall at home, put it in the trunk of my car and set off through the snow from New Rochelle, NY. I actually made it into upper Manhattan before a police officer stopped my car. I explained the problem but he looked skeptical. So, I got out, opened the trunk and produced the diploma. He looked it over closely and broke out laughing. He let me continue on my trip, warning me that I might be stopped again. I wasn't and I arrived on time at the hospital. Having driven around in the snows of Rochester, NY for eight years, I also arrived without a weather-related mishap.

The Speeding Ticket

Some people are just naturally thick, hopefully only occasionally like me. On my way to work while I was still in the ER, a New York State trooper pulled me over on I95 near New Rochelle because I was speeding. By then my car had MD plates and I was dressed in my hospital whites. After the usual license examination and talk about my transgression, the trooper asked me where I was going so fast and why. He asked me two more times and finally gave up and wrote me a ticket. I swear it was weeks later as I was driving my usual route to the hospital (within the speed limit) that I suddenly realized that he was trying to get me to explain that I was on my way to an emergency call at the hospital so that he could give me a warning and not a ticket. I really couldn't blame him for ticketing somebody so dense. He probably remembered my name in case he ever had health related dealings with me.

The Fishing Expedition

In the ER there was a black bag in reserve to be taken along on ambulance calls. There was also a reserve vial of Demerol to be used for pain control if needed. The Demerol was, for security reasons, not kept in the bag but handed to the doctor on his way to the ambulance. One very hot midsummer night not long after I began in the ER a call came in for a woman in labor.

The patrol car collected me after I had placed the Demerol in my white jacket pocket and we proceeded, along with an ambulance, to the tenement to see the about-to-be mother. The apartment was on the fourth floor in a walkup building and, on my way up the stairs, I realized that there was a police officer on every landing. (Later I understood that this was for my protection.) The apartment building was very old and the rooms were immense with high ceilings. All of the windows were open to the courtyard because of the summer heat. Save for the improvised labor room, there was only one piece of furniture to be seen, a straight-backed chair next to a window. I draped my jacket over the chair and went to examine the patient.

Her room was draped with white sheets and she lay in labor on a mattress on the floor. There were children everywhere, some peering over the sheets, very interested in what was going on. The woman was howling. I conducted an exam and decided that there would be time to transport her to the hospital for the delivery.

When I went to retrieve my jacket it was nowhere in sight. As I looked around, an officer handed me my coat with the narcotic vial still in the pocket. The officer patiently explained to me that the chair on which I had hung my jacket was near an open window, that the apartment house tenants routinely fished (literally with fishing poles) items out of such locations. Had my jacket remained where I had left it, it would soon have disappeared Demerol and all. Another mistake I never repeated.

We finally all arrived out on the street where I heard the ambulance attendant say to the patient who was still howling away as she was lifted into the ambulance, "You should close your mouth and cross your legs and if you had done that in the first place this never would have happened!"

Penicillin Please?

Late one evening just after I had begun my first rotation through the Emergency Room, two men literally burst through the door without stopping at the desk to register and hauled me off to the minor OR just across the hall. The next thing I knew I was backed up against the wall inside the room behind the large door. I was frightened at first and then, when bodily harm did not seem to be in the offing, indignant. It seems that these nicely dressed men in their thirties had just returned from an out-of-town convention where they both had contracted gonorrhea! And now they were on their way home to their wives. One of them explained to me that his wife would expect to have him busy in bed as soon as he got home. So, they needed penicillin. Well, there was no way they were going to get it from me! (In any case, it would not have worked instantaneously as they thought it would.) They were not happy and so I thought fast and told them the truth. I reminded them that if I treated them for a venereal disease I would, by law, have to report it and the Department of Health would then take steps to contact all of their sex partners who could be found. That was enough for them to hear and off they went, departing in the same manner that they had arrived. I was unharmed but a bit shaken. It was one of those encounters that I have always wanted to know the outcome of.

The German Sailor

In high school I became something of a German scholar. At least that's what my teacher thought and so I crammed three years of study into two and went on to advanced German in college. But then my other study interests took precedence and between then and post graduate training I had little opportunity to use the language. Except once. There was an accident on board a German ship in New York harbor and an injured sailor who spoke little English arrived in the Emergency Room while I was on duty. I spoke greetings to him in German, much to everyone's relief including his and I was actually able to remember enough to ease him through the emergency treatment and into the hospital. I knew he would have no trouble on the ward since there always seemed to be someone around who could help out with a foreign language. But I was happy to have been of help. The only other time I used my German was in the subway in Berlin, but that is another story.

Cardiac Resuscitations

There I was one evening during my residency covering the ER and the medical wards simultaneously. The emergency call "doctor, doctor" came over the PA system from the ER so that is where I headed at top speed. Indeed, the staff had already begun resuscitation procedures on a man in cardiac arrest. Things were proceeding normally when a second call came from a medical ward that a cardiac arrest had occurred there. I went as quickly as I could to that scene where a bit more intervention on my part was needed. I finally assigned a nurse to man the phone to the ER and continued with the staff which had assembled to treat the patient and to answer questions from the ER at the same time. It seems unreasonable now but at the time I had no sense at all of being stressed. This was work we had been trained to do and even having two arrests going on at the same time didn't occur to me as unfair. Sadly, we eventually lost the man in the ER but the patient on the ward recovered. With cardiac arrests, even today that would not be a bad record.

The Stabbing

One evening when I was an intern I was standing on the parapet where the ambulances pulled up to the ER entrance. It was warm and I was chatting with the chief surgical resident. We watched as across 58th street two men passed each other walking in opposite directions. One kept on going and the other bent over and then looked directly up at us. By that time, the resident was already beckoning the man to come to us. (It struck me later that we should have gone to his rescue, but truly, I did not even know what had happened.) My resident with the experience of many years knew that the man had been stabbed! We helped him into the ER and loaded him fully clothed onto a gurney. As a crowd of nurses and doctors assembled the last I saw was everyone heading speedily toward the elevators up to the operating rooms. The man had sustained an abdominal stab wound but lived to tell about it. I have no idea what his assailant was thinking. I doubt if he was ever seen again except, it being New York City, the men were probably "friends" and eventually met up again.

Early Problems

Having finally figured out how to cross Ninth Avenue without getting killed, I immediately encountered a couple of other problems. My medical school was bordered by an enormous park and an equally enormous cemetery. It was a very quiet place. When I arrived at Roosevelt Hospital in the Hell's Kitchen area of Manhattan on the west side, I had no idea how noisy it would be. I literally heard very little through my stethoscope during my first few days as an intern because of all the street noise. The stick ball games in the street outside my dormitory kept me awake. I eventually adjusted.

Then there were strange diseases and measurements: "appendiceetis", "cholcysteetis", "sauntameters" (centimeters). I always thought "—itis" meaning inflammation was pronounced "eyetis", but I was wrong. In Manhattan, it was pronounced "eetis". It soon became clear to us foreigners that these were affectations of speech and that we had not suddenly encountered diseases that we had never heard of. By the time I had finished my first two years in training the words were being pronounced correctly throughout the medical staff.

Roof Parties

The hospital dormitory had a lovely, flat, tiled roof filling the entire area of the building's footprint with an open area and a glassed in area. It was a great place to relax, have lunch, even to study and a perfect setting for parties. We were repeatedly warned to "keep it down" so as not to bother patients in the adjacent hospital building, so in the evenings we would mostly stay inside the enclosed area.

One party I remember in particular. My wife was about six days past the delivery of our daughter and still a bit sore, but determined to show up at a rooftop party. And we did. I had a bit more to drink than I should have, but before I could even suggest it, Peggy announced that she was not driving home to New Rochelle. So, very early in the morning we set out for home having first to drop off another partyer at his home on the upper west side. It was easy to drive very slowly and inconspicuously in Manhattan and the Bronx. This was not so on the New England Expressway (I95), however. Made no difference to me since I was not about to have an accident. The trip, normally about 50 minutes, took us nearly two hours. The only time I became a bit anxious was passing under the observation bridge near the start of I95. By that time I was probably sober, but I kept on driving at a snail's pace in the far right lane expecting to have the observers send a police car to see what I was up to. They didn't, and we got home without a problem. That was the last time I tried that maneuver. We had had a lot of fun but putting ourselves and others in harm's way was really not very smart.

A New Paging System

About midway through my internship year we were informed that a new paging system was being installed. Eventually we were told to pick up our pagers. They were quite large and could only be transported around if attached to a belt or strap. The hospital extended for one square block and the system would cover that, and with luck, the residence across 58th Street. Now of course one can be paged almost anywhere, but at that time New Jersey was out of the question. We were instructed to have the pager with us at all times. After I spent the first day with my new machine, it came time for me to take a shower before trying to get some sleep. So there I was just ready to get into the shower with my pager in my hand. Then I had to try to find some way to stay in touch so I put it on a ledge in the shower stall. By the time I got back to my room I had fallen out of love with this new devise and never again took a shower with it. Many were the patients however who did not have to listen to the loud speaker paging system any more, and how happy they were!

The Blackout

On November 9, 1965, just as I had one leg in my street pants preparing to go home to White Plains, the lights went out. I used my pocket flashlight to finish dressing and headed for the elevator. The dormitory (which no longer exists) was so old that the elevator was operated by hand by a rope mechanism. No kidding! My car was parked at the corner of 58th Street and Tenth Avenue, and so I was able to reach the corner easily. Someone was already in the intersection directing traffic, since the stoplights were not working. I then made it onto the West Side Highway and was driving along when I suddenly realized that I could not see the lights of New Jersey. I found out the scope of the electrical failure quickly enough on the car radio.

When I arrived home, my wife had three children in the kitchen with her with strict instructions not to wander off. A couple of candles and flashlights were providing some illumination. She was thoroughly annoyed that the lights had gone out and was floored to learn that the entire east coast was in the dark. Still, she managed to produce some sort of meal and we put the kids to bed. We sat in candlelight for awhile and then went to bed ourselves since there was little point in staying up in the dark. By morning I think the problem was resolving since I do not remember missing any time at work.

The wife of one of my professors, however, was certain that she had caused the whole thing since the lights went off just as she turned on the oven. There were many similar stories.

The Bath Blanket

Late one evening when I was an intern, my resident paged me so that I could go with him to see an elderly female patient in a single room on the medical ward. The reason probably was so that I would be able to care for her during the night if the need arose and the resident could get some uninterrupted sleep. In any case, when we arrived in the patient's room, she was sitting up in bed enclosed in an oxygen tent. Her fever was high but not yet in the dangerous range and the nurses wanted to know how this should be dealt with. In those days, bringing the patient's fever down was of paramount concern and the best way to do that was to soak a cotton bath blanket in rubbing alcohol and cover the patient with that. The evaporating alcohol would draw the heat from the patient's body. We agreed that that would be the thing to do and the nurses set to work. When I returned early in the morning to check on things, the little lady was still propped up in her bed, saying her rosary and chortling to herself. She was in great high spirits because she was thoroughly drunk. The alcohol wrap had been left partially under the tent so that she had been breathing in a good deal of alcohol. I would not have been surprised if she had never imbibed alcohol before and had certainly never been drunk. The happy ending—her fever was gone never to return and she was discharged several days later!

The Nametag

In training, we all wore our nametags just above the breast pocket of our white coats. (We also wore shirts and ties!) Several times my nametag resulted in interesting conversations. I was seeing an older man on the private ward, collecting his blood for tests. While I was engaged in my work he suddenly said, having studied my nametag, "Do you belong to the Holland Society?" I indicated that I did not. He then said that in all probability I would be welcome there because of my name. He said he had seen it several times in the Society lists. (A member has to be a direct descendant, in the male line, of someone who lived in or was born in New Amsterdam prior to 1625.) So, we talked for a bit while I told him a few of my family's stories. I really would have been interested had it not been for the $100 fee required to join. That would have been used to verify my qualifications, I suppose. However, at that time I had more important uses for my money. I have looked into the Society from time to time and once even went so far as to obtain membership application forms. The Holland Society is now primarily a philanthropic organization. In the distant past however, one's social climb would have been enhanced and doors of opportunity would have opened for me.

I also went to draw blood on another patient in a private room at the end of a hall where a loudspeaker used for paging people was mounted on the wall just outside his room. As I bent over to do my work, he examined my name tag and loudly said, "So, you're Doctor Hermance!" It startled me, but this time I avoided getting blood all over everything. He told me that he listened all day to people being paged but he had decided that he heard my name the most often. I don't know why that might have been since all of us were pretty busy all the time. Shortly thereafter the new hand-held pager system went into effect.

Mr. Clanfergis

I had occasion to care for an elderly man on the medical ward whom we all referred to as Mr. Clanfergis. He had no relatives that we knew of and he had no visitors from whom we could obtain information. He wore a copper bracelet which, he pointed out to me, had no apparent point of fusion. He said that the bracelet had been fitted onto his wrist when he became the head of the Clan Fergis. He also knew that he would die soon, but not to worry, the Queen of England would pay for his funeral. I saw him daily for many weeks so we became well acquainted.

One day on the ward a nurse came in looking excited and slightly flustered. In fact, she was very nervous because she said she had just mailed a letter to the Queen about Mr. Clanfergis, describing his circumstances as best she could. We all had a good laugh about her action and expected no more to come of it.

A short time later however, the nurse actually received a reply from the Queen's staff saying that our patient was, indeed, the Head of the Clan Fergis and was related to Queen Elizabeth, something like her cousin 22 times removed. The letter also noted that the Crown would not provide funds for any of our patient's care or funeral expenses. We were not surprised, but, when Mr. Clanfergis died, the Explorer's Club in New York City actually did pay for his burial which made us all happy. It turned out that everything our patient had said about himself was true so we were pleased that we had not made fun of any of his claims.

Important People

My training hospital was situated on the west side of Manhattan near Columbus Circle.

Motorcades were frequent in the vicinity. On a cold evening on my way back from supper at a nearby restaurant I stopped to watch JFK's motorcade pass the hospital on 58th Street. There he was as frequently noted in the press waving to everyone while wearing only his business suit. Given what we know now about his general health, one wonders.

Another time, a little farther east toward mid-town Manhattan, I was delighted to watch the Pope ride by on his way to yet another religious gathering I suppose.

On October 4, 1965, my wife and I were privileged to be at Yankee Stadium to hear Pope Paul VI celebrate Mass. We were communicants of St. John the Evangelist parish in White Plains, NY and had recently increased our giving to $1.00 each week from 25 cents. (As a medical resident I was earning about 26 cents an hour.) Our contribution increase had nothing to do with getting tickets to see the Pope. Ever fearless, my wife called the Monsignor Hartigan to see if any tickets for the Mass were still available. To our utter amazement (and amusement) the Monsignor had two tickets which we were able to use. Off we went very happy about our good fortune to an event we will never forget. Thank you Monsignor Hartigan where ever you are!

Another Important Person

Lincoln Center for the Performing Arts was built while I was in training. It was just a couple of blocks away from the hospital on Ninth Avenue. The House Staff at the hospital agreed to be doctors in attendance at performances at the Center. We were given tickets for the performances we were covering, two aisle seats in the last row. So, we were always quick to sign up to cover. Peggy would accompany me and we had great evenings at the theater that way, for free. One night Jackie Kennedy and entourage arrived while I was on duty. I remember her waving to the crowds as she took her center seat down front while facing the back of the theater. (The theater has no center aisle.) It was a medically uneventful evening but ever since I have had fun explaining how at one time I was Mrs. Kennedy's doctor.

The most memorable job I did have at a performance was being called during intermission to the ladies' room. This area seemed palatial and featured very loud, continuous flushing sounds. It seems that my "patient" had fallen off her very high stool at the mirror. Only her vanity was injured, thankfully. Never having been in such a place, the experience was an eye and ear opener for me.

Clutz

My best friend in training was Dick Clutz. He was working in surgery and eventually went on to have a very successful career in surgery in a well-known New England college town. (Once, he even treated my mother-in-law for an infected eye, a stye, while she and Peggy's father were attending a college alumni reunion.) In training we did many things together. Not long after we had begun our internship (PGY1 for the more modern crowd) we went to pick up our paychecks. Even though we were earning about 26 cents an hour at the time, any money coming in was extremely important. At the pay teller's window, I got my check with no trouble. However, the teller informed Dick that the "computer" refused to accept his name. So, no check. As we stood there we all went through any number of possible solutions until we found the right one. The paymaster machine would accept "Klutz"! Dick was able to get paid and he went by that spelling of his name thereafter, getting his check regularly much to everyone's amusement. Dick is anything but a klutz! I have no idea how he was able to cash his checks but I suppose he just endorsed them with his new name.

As usual however, I did not have the last laugh. My father had recently died and so one day when Dick was with me, I was summoned to the medical staff office and presented with a large envelope from our family's lawyer. It contained a copy of my father's last will and testament. At the bottom it said, "The entire estate, 'Hilara B. Hermance'." The remainder, "William E. Hermance, MD". We were sitting on the stairs outside the office at the time and I thought Dick would fall down the stairs laughing.

Santa Claus

I was asked by the nurses to be Santa Claus at their Christmas Party. They had a complete outfit for me, beard and all. I sounded a lot more like Dr. Hermance than Santa, but it was all in good fun. The main thing I remember about that episode was how hot I got in the costume. Now when I see a Santa I wonder just how uncomfortable he is in his red and white outfit.

The Sex Change

I was just out of medical school, an intern, when I went to my usual medical clinic assignment. Had it been a snowy, cold and icy day, all the little old ladies would have been there, but this was in the summer. There was a new patient to see. I walked into the examining room after a brief look at the chart. A nice looking young lady greeted me and I took her medical history. Then I went hunting for a paper hospital gown, having explained that she would have to partially disrobe. When I returned to the room, there she was sitting in a chair by the examining table naked from the waist up. And, she wasn't female. Now I had a nice looking young man for a patient. I was not as good then as I am now hiding my reaction to such surprises but I did the best I could and finished the exam. Neither he nor I mentioned his "sex change" and the visit came to a successful close.

Leprosy

Dr. Freston was the "grand old man" of medicine in my training hospital. We made rounds with him once a week. One day he took us to see a patient on the ward, but in a single room. The patient's wife was attending closely to him and both she and the patient apparently knew Dr. Freston well. The man had the classic "lionine facies" of leprosy but to our eyes was not otherwise deformed. Of course, we all examined him, listened to his heart, etc. until we were treated to his diagnosis. Our attending began to discuss the case in the hallway when suddenly no one but he and I were present. I looked around and said, "Where has everyone gone?" Dr. Freston knew that they had all gone to wash their hands and their stethoscopes. I have never been sure that he appreciated my remaining at his side or simply decided that I was just too dumb to go and wash. After everyone reassembled however, the lesson became clear. Leprosy is a very difficult disease to contract. Dr. Freston pointed out that the patient had been married to the same lady for many years and she had had many children with him. No one saw her taking any particular precautions. I began to feel a little better, but, just in case, I did wash up later on.

The Giraffes

When I arrived at Roosevelt Hospital, the areas for the patients who were unable to pay for medical care, the wards, were still in use. A great many sights, sounds and odors were encountered on the wards which were not present in the private and semi-private areas. One day, while on rounds, we came down from the third floor on our way to the medical ward by way of the gynecology section. The aroma there was quite strong. Without hesitating, my fellow resident and good friend, Chuck, marched up to the first nurse he saw and said, "Which way to the giraffes?" I had to hurry into the hall so as not to burst out laughing in the nurses' station. The place really did smell like the Barnum and Bailey Circus side-show area.

Thankfully, by the time I came out of the Service to resume training, the area had been converted to offices and laboratories and included the first Intensive Care Unit in New York City.

I Never Make a Mistake

Chuck had a droll sense of humor indeed. On rounds one day an elderly woman patient indicated that she thought Chuck had said something in error. He drew himself up to his full 6'2" height and said, "My dear, I haven't made a mistake since 1958, or was it 1957?" Once again I was reduced to laughter. I'm not at all sure that others in attendance "got it".

When We Hear Hoof beats . . .

Many years later after Chuck had become my internist/cardiologist, he prescribed medicine for me. I developed a rash and other symptoms. I knew what it must be but I called him to announce that I had apparently come down with a virus. His comment was, "When we hear hoof beats, we do not think of zebras." I was having a reaction to the medicine, of course.

Years later, I arrived unannounced in Chuck's office complaining of chest pain which had developed while I was driving into New York City. I was just passing his office so I decided to stop there. When he decided that he was sending me to the hospital, I said that I would drive right there. Peering over his glasses, he said, "It is not good form for someone who may be having a heart attack to drive himself anywhere! We will have Peggy come and get you." Thankfully, in the end there was nothing wrong with my heart, but I did endure an overnight in the cardiac care unit.

Neurosurgeon Zapped

I was an intern rotating through surgery when I was asked to assist at brain surgery. Since I was third assistant I stood at the left of the surgeon. My job, I was informed, was to touch the end of the surgeon's probe with a little electric wand which would send an electric impulse down into the probe and cauterize whatever the probe was touching. I had been at that for awhile when suddenly, the surgeon, having received a shock, threw his hand up on the air, dropping the probe. This, of course, was my fault, just as it was the second time it happened. By then, even I was beginning to wonder. With the third shock the surgeon began to examine his glove closely along with all the rest of us. Well, there was a minute tear in his glove on the hand holding the probe. Naturally, he had to rescrub while we waited. All the time I was trying to hide my satisfaction that it had not been my fault and the surgeon deserved this little inconvenience for yelling at me. The patient actually survived quite well despite all the fuss.

The Appendectomy

Also while I was rotating through surgery I was roused one night to go to the operating room. I was told that I was going to perform an appendectomy under close supervision, of course. I don't remember feeling at all nervous about doing this and proceeded to perform the operation to everyone's satisfaction as well as my own. When I went to check on the pathology report however, I was more than a little chagrined. I had removed a normal appendix—someone else's pre-op misdiagnosis. Interestingly, the patient's symptoms subsided immediately thereafter and I heard no more about the case. I have wondered whether the situation was explained to the patient or not. I would have felt obligated to do so but others may not have felt that way. I did learn that sometimes this sequence of events with the symptoms does occur, for which there is no good explanation.

The Lipstick Sign

On one of my earliest hospital rounds we came across a lady on the wards sitting up in bed with her makeup on. After her case was presented, the attending noted that he had not visited her bedside before but that she would be going home soon. He knew that because she had her lipstick on—hence the "lipstick sign"—a sure indication that she was doing well and would soon be discharged. Ever after I have noted how patients took care of their looks, especially the women and, indeed, a little makeup indicates that they are getting ready to go home. Men are likely to start shaving again.

I learned another important lesson when we came upon a woman who would not eat. When asked why since she was doing well otherwise she told us that she was taking 83 pills a day and simply had no appetite. We scrambled to rearrange her medications with the help of the attending, eventually getting things down to about a tenth of that number. She began to eat and shortly went home with the short list of pills. When multiple people write orders this situation can arise. I always remember my partner calling the nursing home in Georgia where his mother-in-law was when he would hear that she was not doing well again. He would get her doctor to review her medications and convince him that certain ones were not necessary. She would invariably improve for a while after his intervention.

Memorable Dinners

One of my professors in training invited a group of us and our wives to dinner at his apartment. His wife, the same woman who thought she had caused the Great East Coast Blackout, produced an all white meal (on purpose). I remember that, indeed, all the food was white and so was everything on the table. Very artistic and very enjoyable. My wife and the hostess eventually became quite friendly and when we would go to the big city allergy conventions she would urge my wife to sit with her in the hotel lobby and "vatch". To this day, my wife and I enjoy watching passersby and so have maintained the tradition.

Another time, my wife and I and several other couples were invited to dinner at the house of one of our colleagues in training. Peggy was pregnant with our daughter. She would get nauseated if she went too long without eating something. She was seated next to a table with an enormous bowl of black olives. Dinner was served very late. At one point I glanced at the olive bowl and saw that they were all gone. There were only a few pits in the bowl. Eventually we made our escape and while we were driving home I asked about the olives. She had eaten them all. When I asked what had become of the pits she produced from her purse a napkin full of olive pits. It would have been embarrassingly obvious that she had eaten them all so she secreted the evidence in her pocketbook!

Purple Penicillin

I was an intern in pediatrics when the case of a little girl who needed penicillin but who was said to be allergic to it was presented to us. She had had penicillin before without trouble. (Of course, it would likely be a subsequent exposure which would cause the problem.) But she had had penicillin since the first exposure without a problem. It was noted that the drug, given orally, was in the form of purple syrup. We contacted the manufacturer who supplied us with the material in the vehicle. (Today, it is hard to get a company to do that because of liability problems.) Sure enough, when the patient was given the syrup alone she reacted to it but she did not react when given penicillin alone. We all thought we were geniuses of course for suspecting this in the first place. The patient recovered fully and went home never to eat anything dyed purple again we hoped.

A Royal Mishap

Back in the day, Roosevelt Hospital maintained an exquisitely furnished suite for VIPs. There were two bedrooms, living room and kitchen. It was all done in pale gray and the walls were carpeted, not wallpapered—the first time I had encountered that. It came my turn to obtain blood from the Duke of Windsor who was staying there with the Duchess for their annual physical exams. In those days, each tube of blood had to be separately attached to the needle already in the vein. One got quite nimble at this after having done "scut work" so often. This time I do not know what happened but half way through this simple procedure, the tube I was using came off of the needle suddenly, spewing the Duke's blood (very red) all over him, the bed, the floor and the wall. I quickly stopped the flow of blood after removing the needle and bolted for the door. By chance, my resident was nearby and I hastily informed him what had happened and announced that I was not going back in to the Duke under any circumstances. I think he understood, but I really didn't care, so embarrassed was I. I never heard any more about the episode—I expected furious kidding from my fellow house staff, but that did not occur. Another time, much later I had occasion to be in the suite and took pains to notice that the "bloody mess" had been skillfully cleaned up.

Post-Coronary

Interns, the lowest of the low, are often given the most undesirable jobs.

One of those was getting a person out of bed after recovery from a heart attack. In my early days, a coronary (myocardial infarction) meant six weeks of absolute bed rest in contrast to today's rapid ambulation. The possibility of complications arising from being in bed so long was always a problem. We would have an IV running and a blood pressure cuff in place. Then we would slowly elevate the patient in bed resting frequently until he was sitting upright. Then we would put his legs over the side of the bed and let him sit there, all the time taking frequent pulse and blood pressure readings as well as inquiring if the patient had any unusual symptoms. Then he would be allowed to stand at the side of the bed, maybe a short walk to a chair. Then the procedure was done in reverse. All of this would take several hours and was quite anxiety provoking. I never had a patient have an adverse event while I was involved though others did. However, I think that all those who survived the initial heart attack eventually got to go home.

The Subway Strike

In 1966, I think, probably in January, the New York City subway workers went on strike. I was driving a little red Volkswagen. We knew that it would be hell-to-pay getting to work and most of the Allergy Department staff commuted on the subway. So I offered to pick up three of them on my way into the City from White Plains. We made careful arrangements about where I would pick them up, etc. It was cold! I got to my first rendezvous successfully. Then it was a very slow drive down through a very congested Manhattan Island. It got colder and colder in the car. I finally picked up all my passengers but it was stop and go traffic and it got even colder in the car. Little did I know that the heater didn't put out warm air unless the engine was running faster than idle which meant that I had to be moving along a little at least. By the time we got to the hospital we were all frozen. But, we had gotten there. Shortly we would be retracing our trip leaving the City, a bit faster this time. For several more days, we repeated this scenario but we knew what the problem was and we were prepared. Everyone was glad to get to work, and it was warm there so the adventure was worth it.

The License Exam

At the end of my first year of training I traveled to Philadelphia, to Temple University Medical School to complete the last part of the exams required for licensure. I went with my friend Dick and we stayed at his house. At Temple we were met by the examiners who would give us our oral exams. A young attending and I went into the chapel which was empty and sat in the last row of pews. He then presented a case to me which involved the lungs and asked how I would proceed to diagnose and treat the condition.

When I had completed my answer he said that I had done well but that I had failed to mention the most important part of the workup. I was at a loss until he reminded me that this was a pulmonary problem and it suddenly hit me that I had not ordered a chest x-ray! I stammered something about assuming that that had been done. He understood completely he said and I eventually passed the examination. I will still bet however that I was not the first or last to leave out the most obvious step for this problem.

"It's a Good Thing I like You"

When I began my post-graduate training, we went to live with Peggy's parents in New Rochelle, my folk's house being too small to accommodate us and the baby. There was a sunroom with its own bathroom just off the entrance foyer. While the baby slept upstairs, Peggy and I borrowed money from her sister to buy a sofa bed, queen sized. Here is where we lived relatively comfortably. We were able to come and go as we pleased without disturbing anyone and were able to see our friends there as well. One evening, we had three other couples over for a social evening, during which I heard one of the four people crowded together on the sofa say to the person next to him, "It's a good thing I like you!"

Another time good friends of ours came for the evening and stayed and stayed. Finally, in the wee hours, Peggy became quite anxious for them to leave and so she suggested to them that she would like to show them how nice our new sofa bed was for us. She herded us all into the front hall and opened the bed. There was literally no way three of us could get back into the room and Peggy did not offer to close up the bed. So we stood and talked for a while in the hallway and our friends finally left. Lo these many years later we are all good friends still.

The White Pants Syndrome

Several of my classmates took an extra year in medical school to pursue special interests. Some interns and residents however, seemed never to finish training. This was called "The White Pants Syndrome" in which, it was speculated, the wearer was so anxious about leaving the protected learning environment of training that they put off doing so as long as possible, wearing hospital whites all the time. Not so with me, but being eager to get going on my career led to another complication. About a week before I finished training, my wife asked me what I planned to wear to the office since I had nothing much else than white pants and jackets to wear. I did not have a suit or reputable sport outfit with which to start practice. There wasn't much money handy either, but I did manage to put a couple of outfits together to open my practice.

As I started my practice at the same time as Medicare/Medicaid began, I never saw any problem with the system. But, we sure did hear about how awful everything would be in the future from our attendings who were used to the old fee-for-service style. They all eventually adjusted!

The Condom

To celebrate the completion of my training, Peggy and I decided to do something special. Since we had about $800.00 in the bank, which would not get us very far for everyday living, and since a cruise to the Bahamas from New York in those days cost about the same amount, we decided to blow our bank account on a cruise.

Also in those days one was allowed to have guests come onto the ship to see one off. And so we entertained some people in our cabin. One of the guests was a resident in Urology.

When we received our table assignments on board, the two couples who joined us each had been give two bottles of wine as had we. And so we arranged to have one bottle each night of the cruise for our table. We had a wonderful time with these people for an entire week. On our last night, the bottle of wine which my urologist friend had given to us was produced along with a card, which did feel a bit thicker than a normal small card would. All unsuspecting, however, I tore open the envelop and watched in shock as a red and white Trojan condom flew across the room! What a stir that caused. On the line the next morning waiting to disembark, one of our tablemates announced that as they were getting ready to leave the ship, they discovered a gross of condoms hidden in a dresser drawer. It had been slipped in there by his boss at their boarding party.

The Military Years

Staten Island

It came time for me to undergo a physical exam preparatory to joining the Public Health Service (an arm of the Coast Guard) as part of my Berry Plan obligation for military service. To do this I had to go to Staten Island by ferry to the huge Public Health Hospital there. Everything went along quite well until I was leaving. Loping down the steps behind me calling my name was a hospital aide asking me to stop and waving an x-ray envelope around. I managed to see written on the folder "Do Not Show to Patient". That was a little scary. I was shown into the radiologist's office then and we both peered at my chest x-ray. It looked OK to me. The doctor pulled his centimeter ruler out and measured the width of my heart. Then he announced that my heart seemed to be within normal size limits after all and I proceeded on my way home.

Several days later, I got a notice asking me to reappear at the hospital because there were red blood cells in my urine. Immediately, I remembered that I had given the specimen directly after a digital rectal exam, which even I knew might push some red blood cells into my urine. Of course, upon examination of the new specimen the results were normal.

My wife accompanied me on this second trip via the Staten Island Ferry. She suddenly disappeared from my side. I found her on the other side of the ferry peering intently at the Statue of Liberty. I was hardly able to believe that she had never before seen the Statue in person since she grew up just a few miles away in New Rochelle, NY. That was indeed the case, bearing out the idea that one tends to ignore the "local" sights.

The Pentagon Calling

In my second year of residency, I was all ready to go to my assignment at The Medical Center for Federal Prisoners in Springfield, Missouri, when Peggy announced to me one day at home that the Pentagon was calling. She thought this was hysterical, but I thought there might be a problem. The caller asked if I would be interested in putting off my departure to Springfield for a year at which time I would be assigned to the Federal Prison in Atlanta as Chief of Medicine. I allowed that this was a fine offer (I had no idea about rank at the time) but that I had no money and I had to go into the service right away in order to feed the family. The caller was quite sympathetic and did not press the issue, thankfully.

So, I missed out on that offer, but, soon after I arrived at the hospital in Springfield, my Colonel called me into his office, handed me his own oak leaf clusters from the top drawer of his desk and announced that I was now a Major. It seems that I had been made Chief of Medicine at the Medical Center and that, in order to become a department chief I had to be a Major. So, I was promoted on the spot and, of most interest to me, began earning more money. The irony of the promotion in view of the earlier offer was not lost on anyone!

Missouri Move

When the van driver showed up to load our meager belongings for the move from New Rochelle, NY to Springfield, MO, where I would be putting in my military time, he commented on how glad he was to be going to the Midwest since in all likelihood he would not have to cart furniture up stairs. (This was true in our case.) He left on Thursday afternoon, July 1st. We left the next morning with two babies and another on the way. We crossed the Mississippi River in St. Louis on Route 66 in mid-afternoon on Sunday. It was terribly hot and there was no air conditioning in the car and practically no one else on the road. The highway around St. Louis was very wide. We were stopped at a red light when I noticed my wife talking to someone out of her window. And there he was, our van driver. Peggy said that she guessed that he would not have to call us in the morning before unloading for us, but rules were rules and he would have to call. Of course, had we planned this rendezvous it never would have happened. Later that day, we all piled into our motel on the side of a hill overlooking the highway. The kids got out to the pool as fast as they could just in time to wave at the passing moving van. The driver tooted as he flew by on the road.

On Monday, July 4th, we had just settled down in bed after an exhausting day finishing moving with two kids when were treated to a loud "Mooo" from the field behind us. We both burst out laughing, deciding that we suburbanites were truly in the country now.

The Stop Sign

When we arrived in Springfield, having driven down Route 66, my car was very dirty. I knew that I would need to obtain Missouri license plates within a short time after my arrival. On my route to the prison there was a stop sign that I negotiated every day. I was always in uniform. It occurred to me that whoever saw me with my New York MD license plates and dirty car would assume I had just come off the highway and would not think that I was a Missouri resident. So, I reasoned, I would just leave the car dirty and I could thereby avoid the license plate hassle. One day, after I had come to a full stop and was proceeding on I saw a police car with lights flashing behind me. Clearly I was the object of pursuit. I pulled over knowing that I had not run the stop sign. The officer walked up to my car and said, "Doc! You are going to have to obtain Missouri license plates." He then advised me that he had seen me go by many, many times. I and my dirty car had become a source of amusement for him, but, enough was enough.

The story continues. I arrived shortly thereafter at the DMV and stood on a long line. Finally, I got up to the counter whereupon the clerk asked if I had all my papers in order. What papers I wondered. So, I returned home, donned my formal service uniform, hat and all, and reappeared on another long line. A clerk at a station that wasn't open spied me and beckoned me over to her place. I patted my jacket pocket when asked about my papers. Since it was apparent to her that I had no idea about "papers" she filled them out for me. She asked when I had come into the state to live and when I gave the real date she said, "Oh, no, no. That will never do." So I gave another date about 3 months later. "Much better," she said. I was now within the law. I was directed to the eye test area, passed that and left with a new set of Missouri plates.

About a month later, New York State asked to have my old plates returned. I know not why. Luckily, I still had them in the trunk and mailed them back to New York. When I returned to New York, I had to do all this over again but it was not so easy without my uniform!

The Escape

One of the first stories I heard upon my arrival at the prison was about an inmate who escaped. He stole a car from the driveway of the house nearest to the entrance to the prison grounds. There were two cars there, a black Ford and a white sports car. Naturally, he stole the flashy car. He was finally arrested on the Pennsylvania Turnpike after the car was spotted from a police helicopter. Had he stolen the Ford, he would probably still be at large. When I asked about escapes sometime later, my Colonel noted that when one has every day for many years to think up ways to escape it is not surprising that sometimes a prisoner actually does.

A Moving Experience

Dr. C. was a surgeon at the Medical Center. He also ran the dermatology clinic. When he finished with each prison inmate he always said, "Go, and sin no more!" This amused all of us greatly.

Dr. C. had been a physician in an Italian section of Boston. One night arriving home, he was so exhausted that he pushed himself up the stairs on his rear end. By the time he got to the top of the stairs he had decided to quit private practice and to join the Public Health Service. He had had a very large practice and maintained a huge house filled with antiques, oriental carpets, inlaid wooden pieces and paintings. He and his wife had no children. So, he wound up in Springfield awaiting the arrival of household goods to be installed in the very large house he would live in while at the prison. Early on we were all invited to his house for a party. I was puzzled by the fact that there was so little furniture visible. Here a chair, there a rug, an occasional lamp was all. It seemed that on the trip to Springfield, the moving van fell off a bridge into a creek. Since it was a military move, all the damage was fully covered by insurance. One can hardly imagine the cost of repairing all the furniture, but it had to be done, soaked rugs treated, veneers repaired, etc. Thus, every so often a repaired piece would arrive at Dr. C.'s house to be placed just where it was meant to go. Eventually it all got done but it took a year or more.

A Southern Friend in a Small World

On my very first day at the prison, the incoming group of officers was being shown around the premises. At one point I found myself alone with another doctor, Dr. Dan Dunaway while we waited for an elevator to return for us. He looked at me and said, "Did you mash da button?" It took me a moment to decipher this remark and I replied that I had indeed pushed the button. Dan's family and ours became very good friends while we worked together. He kidded me, among many other things, about the teabag that I often carried in my breast pocket. And I kidded him about his accent. Several years later when we were planning to visit the Dunaways in Memphis, Dan's wife Virginia said that when we got there she would have some friends in to sit around and listen to us two talk! Virginia grew up in Magnolia, Arkansas—pretty southern if you ask me—and I eventually took care of a very generous White Plains Hospital benefactor who had also grown up in Magnolia and knew Virginia's family.

Another time, in Bath in England, Peggy and I were having tea next to a table where two ladies were seated. Striking up a conversation, we discovered that they were from Memphis and that while they did not know Dr. Dunaway, they surely did know Virginia who by then was greatly involved in Memphis affairs.

Eventually, over their southern parents' objections (the grandchildren might become northerners) the Dunaways wound up for a while in Indianapolis. We still visit one another and continue to enjoy kidding each other.

A Psychiatric Friend

Another friend of mine, Alan, was a psychiatrist. His wife was the daughter of Sigmund Freud's medical doctor who had fled to America and became a psychiatrist. He insisted that if Alan was to marry his daughter he would have to be psychoanalyzed. Then, Alan decided to become a psychiatrist which required another psychoanalysis. Finally, he wanted to become a child psychoanalyst and for this he needed to be psychoanalyzed again. (His wife usually underwent psychotherapy each time her husband was psychoanalyzed, presumably to help her cope with whatever changes to his personality the analyses produced.) Alan's comment? "Anyone who has to be psychoanalyzed three times ought to have his head examined!"

Once, while Peggy was in labor, Alan accompanied me to the dentist for a root canal. He insisted the whole time that I was experiencing "sympathetic labor pain." I wasn't. Sadly, this lovely man and excellent young physician died only a very short time after we left the service.

During Peggy's labor this time with George, she had a very prolonged and difficult time. I declined the opportunity to be present in the delivery room. I was surrounded by Alan, the neighbor lady and Peggy's mother when Dr. Bonebrake, the obstetrician, arrived to say to me that they were having some trouble. He whispered all of the sentence except the last word which everyone heard. I asked what the problem was and he replied that he couldn't get the baby out! Finally, he had to resort to a medium forceps delivery. When I was summoned to the nursery, I spotted our pediatrician just leaving which frightened me. He had been called in to see if he could detect any damage to the baby, the most likely being compression of the facial nerve from the forceps. There was none and George, our real Ozark hillbilly, was safe and sound.

Dr. Bonebrake, the obstetrician also delivered his first set of triplets that day. There were two observation windows available in the nursery. The weight of the triplets was not equal in total to George's weight, so, naturally, the nurses displayed them in one window and George in the other window complete with the weights of each. My wife refused to view her new baby while there were people there adding up the weights and pointing and laughing over George (11 pounds, 2 ounces) Thus the problem with the delivery. The nurse assisting, a nun, won a case of beer from the doctor for guessing closest to our new baby's weight.

Popovers

The wife of one of the couples we were in service with liked to entertain, as did we. Early on, Patt had some of Peggy's famous popovers which she made by the recipe and which she gave to Patt. The popovers were and still are divine when she makes them. Practically every time thereafter when we would have dinner at Patt's house, she produced popovers. They varied from impossible to fair. On the last time we dined together at their house, Patt once again produced popovers, wonderful ones, just like Peggy's. When asked how she had achieved this result, she said that she had followed the recipe (finally) to a tee and thus the excellent result.

On our first visit to Patt and Fred's house there was a pretty little girl running around. This was their biological daughter. They told us however that there would be no more natural children because of Fred's low sperm count. This was thrown into casual conversation—Peggy and I tried not to look non-plussed. Indeed, they did later adopt a boy. Unfortunately, Fred died shortly thereafter. It was a terrible loss, Fred being a great guy and excellent psychiatrist. Patt went on to be a sex therapist associated with the Masters and Johnson Clinic at the University of Indiana. We are still in frequent touch by card, email and occasional visits. (And we manage to go with the flow with Patt without appearing surprised.)

A Cuban Friend

One of the other doctors at the prison was a Cuban expatriate, Dr. Salas. His English was very good but not perfect. We all eventually got used to "hed-achee" meaning "headache" and "aviabale dosache" meaning "available dosage."

Vietnam

At the prison medical center I had occasion to hear about the Vietnam War in its earliest stages, in part because I had very high security clearance. Before hostilities got underway, there were soldiers being dropped into the country to see what was what. They were left for up to six months and then picked up by helicopter. I thought how lucky I was to have my "cushy" job, but I followed developments with great interest

The Birdman.

During my years as Chief of Medicine at the Medical Center for Federal Prisoners I took care of the Birdman of Alcatraz. He had been transferred to Springfield when the prison at Alcatraz was closed. At the Medical Center he did not do any avian research and he lived in the general population. He came often to my office mostly I think, to chat since he was in apparent good health, in his seventies. He wore his trademark green eye shade.

Remarkably, even though some of his research on birds was a hoax, using the laboratory provided by the government at Alcatraz, he also made some lasting discoveries which are still to be found in ornithology books. He even made some money all of which he spent for legal representation in his many courtroom skirmishes over the years.

Robert Stroud, the "Birdman", was a federal prisoner because he killed a man, whom, as the story has it, he found in bed with his girlfriend. Alaska was still a United States territory and so his crime was a federal one. Hence, he was sentenced to the federal prison at Alcatraz. Then, near the time he would have been released, he killed a prison guard. Because of that he was sentenced to life in federal prison.

By the time I met him, plans were underway to have him released to live with a woman in Oklahoma. Except for visits to court with his lawyers and watching television, he had no knowledge of the outside world, so that careful attendance on him was deemed necessary for his survival after his release. Unfortunately, he never made it out of prison. He died of a heart attack one night in November, 1963. I was summoned to the hospital, pronounced him dead and arranged for an autopsy in two day's time.

Many years later, "Squeaky" Fromme took a pot shot at President Gerald Ford. My oldest son was in high school and the class assignment for the next day was to find out what everyone's parents were doing when President Kennedy was assassinated. My son asked his mother first at the dinner table. She replied that she had just hung up the phone after talking with Mrs. Dunaway and was on her way back to the kitchen when she heard the news. "Oh, never mind," was my son's response. Then he asked me what I had been doing. I said that I was doing an autopsy on the Birdman of Alcatraz when the assassination took place. He looked wide eyed at me and said to his mother, "He can't have made that up that fast!" And, indeed, I hadn't made anything up.

While I was standing with the Medical Director and the Chief of Surgery at the autopsy table, an announcement about President Kennedy came over the intercom. We were shocked of course, but my Colonel indicated later that at least now Paris Match and many other news services would stop calling him at all times of day and night about the Birdman's demise. He never got another call on that subject.

And my son had the most startling story to tell in class the next day!

The end of the story is that, mercifully, I was on leave when Burt Lancaster showed up to begin his preparation for the movie "The Birdman of Alcatraz".

Christmas Cards

A very sad moment for me came during my service on the acute medical ward in the prison hospital. One day, checking on the patients, I found myself in an old timer's room. It was Christmastime and there were several Christmas cards taped to the wall. I commented on them to the patient who told me that they were from his children. Later, I learned that each year the patient, a lifer, sent himself cards, put them up and explained where they came from to anyone who asked. I am quite sure that he had long since lost any connection with his family and this was his way of dealing with the loss.

Mickey Cohen

While he was a prisoner in the Federal Penitentiary in Atlanta, Mickey Cohen, famous bad person, had his head bashed in as part of a contract on his life. After initial treatment there, he was sent to the prison in Springfield mainly to be kept under observation and to recover as much as he could. It turned out that he recovered remarkably well. Around this time two books came out about gangsters in one of which Cohen was written about. One day I accompanied him down the hall while he was carrying one of these books. I picked the wrong title to ask him about and his reply was that he most certainly was not reading that book because that one was about "criminals"!

Once, while Cohen was a prisoner at the hospital, he had a visitor. This rarely happened on the wards and was always preceded by a "heads up" from security. Not this time though, for some reason. I came out of my office heading for the elevator when I encountered an unescorted, tall, shapely and very pretty woman. She looked slightly disoriented and so I asked what her business was there. She had come to see Cohen and proceeded to have a visit with him in a closely observed area. Later, Cohen was paroled and, I presume, was able to take up with his girlfriend once again. The lady in question starred in a 1977 movie. She has been quoted as saying that she was Mickey Cohen's girlfriend. She eventually went to jail for failing to "snitch" on the Mob and wrote a book about her experiences. She streaked Hollywood Boulevard once during the height of the "streaking" fad when she was in her 50s.

The Salute

One hot summer morning in Springfield I was on my way into the prison wearing my summer tan uniform and carrying my brown paper bag lunch. As I neared the wide stairs that led up to the main entrance, (a government building like so many others with a wide expanse of steps and an imposing façade), a taxi pulled up to the steps. Without looking I knew that several guns were trained on the vehicle. (No guns were used in the prison, the guards were unarmed. But the perimeter area was closely watched from the guard towers in this maximum security prison facility.) Out hopped a young man, a Marine in full dress uniform. Spotting me, he snapped to attention and to my astonishment, saluted. I had never been saluted before and I had no idea what to do so I casually sort of waved at him, touching the brim of my hat. He continued to stand at attention. When I got near enough to him to ask he said that he was there to visit his brother. And I offered this piece of advice as we climbed the stairs, "Please, whatever you do, don't salute anyone while you are visiting here!" It seems amusing to me now but as far as I knew, no one on duty would have had the faintest idea how to respond to a salute.

An Uneven Count

Each year at the medical center the staff underwent a physical exam given assembly-line style by the staff physicians. The first time I was involved it fell to me to do hernia checks on about 48 men. I didn't find any hernias. During the discussion afterwards of what abnormalities had been found, I felt it my duty to inform the others that I had had to examine only 95 testicles. To this day I am amazed at the dropped jaws and the time it took these doctors to understand just what my efforts had discovered.

Mumps

It seems that I never had the mumps as a child.

When I was in the service we lived in a small ranch house near the prison hospital. One day at sunset I was in the room that we used as a playroom for the children when my oldest son stood up. He was silhouetted in the west facing window. One look was all it took—I called to my wife to announce that Billy had the mumps. The outline of his swollen parotid glands was clearly visible.

The next day I thought it best to stop in at my Colonel's office before going up to the medical ward to tell him about my son. After I did so, he told me to go home because it was clear to him that I had the mumps, too. So, home I went to develop enormous swelling of my parotid glands so that my face came to resemble a football. I remember shaving without the usual facial topography. I also remember the pain that would develop in my jaws if I even heard my wife fixing a meal in the kitchen. I called my internist to ask what was to be done, knowing that I would just have to suffer through. His comment was, "Call me back if it 'goes down'." I got a lot of that including from my dear friend and neighbor, the prison Protestant Chaplain who kept asking me if it had "gone down yet." I think he thought this was very funny, but to me it wasn't. In any case, my groin was unaffected.

Eventually the other two kids came down with the disease. It soon became evident who among our friends had had the mumps and who had not. Many came to visit but there were notable exceptions among the "haven't hads". They were taking no chances. I can't say I enjoyed my sick leave, but we all recovered without sequelae.

The Back Brace

At the medical Center we had small medical conferences in the radiology department. Early on I noticed a back brace hanging on a clothes stand in the corner of our meeting room. It was covered with dust, clearly not having been worn for a very long time. A few months into my first year there, the Cuban missile crisis developed. The night that our troops were being moved about the country, an old friend, an obstetrician at Ft. Hood, Texas, called to say that he was being sent to Georgia for possible deployment. I was shocked. I was not happy about the prospect of that happening to me. The next day I found that my commanding officer had had similar thoughts. Upon entering the X-ray area, I immediately noticed that the back brace was missing. When the Colonel arrived a little later, it was apparent that he was wearing the brace. He had no intention of being sent anywhere. However, he did have to endure some good-natured kidding. Happily, the Cuban problem was resolved without anyone having to go to war. (We never did figure out why an obstetrician would have been needed.)

Christmas with Marianne

While I was in the service, my Colonel and I became very good friends. After I was discharged we began to receive Christmas greetings from him and his wife Marianne. After the Colonel died, we continued to hear from Marianne and still do to this day. Every letter was the opposite of the usual Christmas note. One son is in jail, both grandsons are drinking again and one is in jail, I need gall bladder surgery, we have had to move, etc., etc. These are long letters which invariably left us laughing. They are all the more amusing because they are all true and not at all tongue-in-cheek. In this year's letter Marianne noted that her family thinks she is an ATM machine! A real regret is that we didn't save all of the letters. They would have made a wonderful collection for a Christmas gift book. Marianne, with her dry sense of humor and straight face would get a kick out of that.

Gladiolas

Our small rental house in Springfield had an enormous backyard. To one side and a little away from the house was a round patch of ground which never had any grass on it. It seemed to me to be the perfect spot for a small garden so I planted a great many gladiola bulbs there. They bloomed beautifully for two years despite some very cold winter weather. Just before our departure as I was leaving the service I gathered up all the beautiful blossoms and we took them to my Colonel's house where we had been invited for dinner. The aforementioned Marianne was thrilled to have so many lovely flowers gracing her very large house.

While I was in the yard collecting the glads the neighbor lady noted how pretty they were and what a shame it was to have to cut them down. I commented on how nicely they had survived and flourished. She explained this to me by revealing that the bare spot in the lawn was above the septic tank and was therefore warm all the time. Who knew?

Leaving the Service

Now it had become time for us to move back to New York to resume my residency. We had had very pleasant neighbors while in Missouri and we knew we would be very homesick after leaving. (My wife was in tears half way to St. Louis.) This was a military move and so we expected very little trouble from it. However, the movers did not show up until late in the day. We had to leave that day since we had been renting the house and I was on a tight schedule for getting back to work. It became obvious that there was no way that the van could be loaded before nightfall. So we had the house emptied onto the front lawn, locked the doors, said goodbye to our neighbors, all of whom were assembled on the lawn by then, too, and left. Our friends promised to watch over the move and the movers for us. If everything we owned had not been on the front lawn and we had been happy to be leaving, the whole thing would have been funny. As it was, everything, including us, arrived intact in New York several days later. Two pillows went missing during the move about which we grumbled a bit, only to find them a couple of years later when we moved once again. Our oldest son still remembers this whole operation.

Protection?

I had not been out of the service very long, just getting settled with three small kids, when a letter arrived from an inmate at the prison insisting that I appear in Colombia, South Carolina to testify in his favor about a criminal matter. I knew that was not going to happen before I read any further, but the end of the letter was alarming. The letter writer ended with a wish for the continued good health of my wife and children. That sent a chill down my spine and I immediately called my former Colonel at the prison. He went over the possible threat with me and asked me to forward the letter to him. Finally he said that visible protection in the person of federal government agents would be at my disposal immediately. All I needed to do was to give him the OK. So, I asked his advice. He said that no threats like these had been carried out and he did not think that protection would be necessary. Thankfully, he turned out to be right.

One night about six months later a man who had worked in the x-ray department at the prison with whom I had had a pleasant working relationship and who had recently been paroled showed up at the emergency room in New York City asking for me. For some reason, I remember that he was wearing formal patent leather shoes but was otherwise normally dressed. I gave him the names of some people to see at the hospital about a job. He left into the nighttime city and I never saw him again.

The Jackass

Her parting comment was, "You'll be receiving a jackass in the mail."

A physician, Frank and his family whom I met in the service came to live with us in White Plains for about six weeks. He was studying at the previously mentioned Public Health Hospital on Staten Island, and then would be moving on to finish his radiology residency. We were all good friends and our kids loved having more playmates. Frank's wife Anne had made a set of beautiful bisque manger scene figurines which she gave to us as a thank you for letting them stay with us. However, she had not completed the set and thus her parting words. Not long after, the donkey figurine arrived. We are still using this set 40 years later on our mantel at Christmas, carefully hiding the figure of Baby Jesus until Christmas Day. The kids of course, cannot let me forget the year that I could not remember where I had hidden the figurine!

The Practice Years

In the Office

Smelling Salts

The floors in the White Plains office were linoleum tiles over concrete. On the rare occasions when a patient would pass out (vaso-vagal syncope), it was obvious that it was going to happen long enough beforehand to get the patient recumbent before he fell. One day, however, as I was beginning skin testing on a pediatric patient, I heard a thud behind me. Mama had passed from the scene. (The patient in the meantime had had his nose in my way trying to watch the shots he was getting.) Out came the smelling salts which were always on the examining table, to help revive the lady. They worked just as they were supposed to and fortunately she did not sustain any injury. After that we kept smelling salts in other places as well, closer to the treatment rooms, just in case.

Losing Count

A lot of counting goes on in an allergy practice. The number and identity of allergens is especially important with skin testing. Once, while my nurse and I were doing passive transfer tests on a patient's back, a bad thing happened. There were about 30 tests, the sites for them had been prepared and numbered and I was placing the antigen tests in the prepared sites. My nurse, a crackerjack worker not prone to errors, suddenly said the two most dreaded words in medicine, "Oh, oh!". In this case it was not a dreaded finding but only her reaction to the fact that she had lost count of the tests and therefore, about halfway through, lost the identity of one or two of the antigens. Luckily, we were able to salvage most of the exercise. The patient was none the wiser, his diagnosis and treatment were unaffected, but my nurse was mortified. I never kidded her about the episode, however, because I knew how upset she had been.

Office Finances

Often the last thing the office manager would say as I was on my way out the door on Friday afternoons was either, "You can throw another meatball in the spaghetti tonight." or "No extra meatballs tonight." In the first case, the office receipts for the week were good. The second meaning is obvious.

Once, however, a man showed up in the office and announced that he would like to review our telephone records. He would, he said, for a percentage of the refund, be able to get money because the phone company had undoubtedly overcharged us. We agreed and soon had $8000.00 (!) in refund money. About five years later, he showed up again, but this time we only got $5000.00 since the records had not extended over such a long period.

However, other complications arose. We got a letter out of the blue stating that New York City thought that our suburban office was a sham office and that therefore we owed taxes to the City on the basis of the entire income to the practice. It cost us several thousand dollars in lawyer fees to get that straightened out only to have this happen again a few years later. This time inspectors came to see if we really did have a second working office. We used to carry charts back and forth to the New York City office when patients wanted to see us there. So, much to our surprise, the agents asked to see three specific charts. (How they knew these patients were seen in the White Plains office was never clear to us. We began to believe in Big Brother!) As luck would have it, 2 of these charts had been transferred to the NYC office! They duly noted the one chart we did have, and, I guess, saw what was clearly a functioning office, and so this time we incurred no legal expenses. We never heard another word from the tax people again.

When the HMOs started up, we were required to prove that we had offices. I mean, the HMOs weren't nutty enough already! This was determined by having an inspector come to see the office. The visits were never very long—all they were interested in knowing was whether we had a functioning bathroom!

Gifts

From time to time while I was in training I would hear about the occasional gifts patients would give to doctors. A baby grand piano here, a trip to an exotic locale there. I never really understood that since the fees were all paid as well. However, over the course of my career I have received many gifts, not grand to be sure, but still very pleasing. One man would bring me a beautiful tie and matching handkerchief every few months, far more expensive than I would consider an appropriate price for such things. I still wear some of them. The label on the ties amused my friends—it advertised the New York Heating Company. No fashion label for this patient! I received limited edition prints which I still have in my house, one museum quality modern painting, small statuary, including a beautiful cast iron girl holding high a balloon, really a ping pong ball, and even an original collection of Jewish jokes given to me when I retired, by the collector, the husband of one of my favorite patients. I have even received lovely gifts from patients after I retired, including a set of Tiffany champagne glasses, a coffee table-type gardening book and another all about roses. I still really don't get it, but it's nice to know that people feel so well disposed toward me.

On TV

I have even been on TV a few times, the most recent in a story about allergies on local TV in Philadelphia. Once while on a TV call-in medical show, a listener wanted to know if it was OK for him to take an antihistamine before going out drinking since he had a problem with some wines. It was hard for me to keep from spluttering my emphatic "No!" My career in radio and television actually began when I was in high school (I can't remember why now) but clearly did not evolve into a highly lucrative career.

Jokes

Over the years I saw patients who loved to tell me jokes—almost all new to me. I tried to remember some of the best ones, but I might hear so many in a day that it was hard to keep track. By far, the best joke tellers were women, one in particular, Trudy, who heard the stories at her bridge games. And they were raunchy and she couldn't wait to try them out on me. I also had a Jewish patient whose husband I got to know and who told particularly Jewish jokes. The week I retired, a long-time patient came in for her treatment and handed me a book-length folder of jokes which her husband had collected. He wanted me to have a copy. I was touched by the gesture. Another patient, an elderly Irishman this time and a severe asthmatic, always came prepared with a story or two. His jokes ranged from ethnic through just plain smutty, and, since he spoke with a booming voice, I always saw him behind closed doors, or, at least got up and closed them if he indicated a story was forthcoming. My friends often wanted to know where I got all my stories (the ones I dared to tell) and they would nod knowingly when I said that I heard them from my patients.

Shooting Up

My wife and I had dear friends who were a black couple with two children. The mother had also been a patient for awhile when her son became a patient as well. He was a very tall, gawky teenager at the time. His mother was a stunning beauty. As I frequently called the patients in from the waiting room myself, I always got a kick out of this lady saying to her son, "OK, let's go in and shoot up together!" This invariably brought surprised if not shocked looks from the other people in the waiting room.

Mr. Universe

A young man, a former Mr. Universe, came to see me in White Plains. He was a pleasant patient. But, when I went to place some skin tests in his upper arm, I couldn't help but comment that I was unlikely to run out of room for the tests. His upper arm was as big around as my thigh, and I am not a small person.

College Kids

I was bemoaning the fact that I had 3 children in college at the same time to a patient in White Plains who was the CEO of an international firm situated in Westchester County. I knew that if one listened hard enough from the waiting room that conversations in one of the treatment rooms in the office could be faintly overheard. In addition, we called all patients out of the waiting room by title and last name (a practice apparently forbidden in the South). The patient noted that he had five children in college at that point! Why five? It seems he had adopted his brother's children after his brother and his wife had been killed in a car accident. His kids were all about the same age whereas mine were not and I would not have three in school except for one year. The amusing part came when the next patient, a woman, came into the treatment room and announced that seeing as who he was he could surely afford to pay for five kids in college at the same time! And, she was right.

Cat Stories

Both of these tales are rather sad.

Very early on in my practice, I tested a little girl for possible cat allergy. She was highly positive, cat immunotherapy was not very good at the time and so I advised, as usual, that eliminating the cat from the household would be the wisest course, if not the only the reasonable one. The little girl's mother announced that the cat was hers and that the little girl would have to go. My secretary heard the pronouncement and later told me that she had all she could do to keep from interrupting the conversation to give the mother a well-deserved piece of her mind. So, the little girl, about 9 years old, was sent to live with her grandmother in an animal-free household to overcome her problem, and, presumably to live happily ever after.

A similar story came up not long thereafter, but in this case, a slightly older girl already knew what the problem was, confirmed by testing, and begged her mother to let her go to live with her grandmother. The mother readily agreed. This mother might have been able to make sufficient adjustments in the home environment to accommodate her daughter and the cat, but we never knew since the child went to live elsewhere. From these two stories I learned a lot about the lengths people will go to to retain their relationship with their animals and afterward I was less often taken aback when similar problems arose.

The Christmas Tree

There was a young girl who would now be called a tween, who had asthma. She knew that she had more trouble with her breathing whenever there was a real Christmas tree in the house. One night, she took the situation into her own hands. Having enough sense to drag the tree, fully decorated, through the front door bottom first, she deposited it on the lawn outside and went back to bed. I thought that she had behaved terrifically well. Her parents got the message.

A Red-headed Girl

Often patients would park their cars on a side street opposite my White Plains office. To get back and forth they had to cross a very busy road leading into town. One day, I had given shots to a pretty young girl with a massive amount of curly red hair. After she left the office with her mother, we thought we heard sirens, but the office was situated in such a way as to insulate us from street noises. We learned that upon crossing the road, my patient was struck by a car. It turned out that, though she was known to have hit her head on the hood of the car in the accident according to her mother who saw the whole thing, she was saved from a very serious impact by her bountiful red hair which acted a cushion for her head. She did, however, fracture her pelvis, for which she spent some time in the hospital. I visited her, of course, and her family, and made arrangements for her mother to park next to my office door in future. When I think of it now, it was a wonder that in over thirty years, no one else from my practice was ever injured crossing the White Plains Post Road.

A Red-headed Lady

While I was still working for my professor, whose partner I would soon become, I met a fascinating lady. She had been a patient for awhile. She had henna-dyed hair, done up in various startling ways and often wore outlandish makeup and clothes. She was tall and stately, especially in her high heels. She spoke in a very formal way to everyone, though I knew she was not snobbish. I always used her last name when I addressed her. I would often meet her on my way across town to the office since she lived in an area on the West Side near Columbus Circle through which I passed almost daily. I remember her initially because she would arrive in the office carrying a box of Kleenex tissues. She had such severe allergic rhinitis that she was never without the tissues. Eventually I knew we were making progress with her therapy because she did not always have her Kleenex with her. Eventually she was able to go about without her tissues at all. I remember reminiscing with her about the Kleenex when, years later we would meet on the street. We would both have a chuckle over that.

The Yellow Tie

For many years we employed a female allergist to help us in the office. She was a Holocaust survivor, educated in Vienna and the USA. Her English was impeccable, but she did have a slight accent. One day I arrived in the office wearing a bright yellow tie. She took one look and exclaimed, "Oh, you're wearing your cannery tie!" I subsequently figured out that she meant "canary" tie. We had a good laugh and ever after when anyone wore yellow in the office, we would refer to the color as "cannery".

Rotary Phones

My office had to be one of the last to obtain touch-tone phones. Kids would come in for their shots and then, after waiting the prescribed time, ask to call their parents for a ride home. My secretary, who got a charge out of it, would invite them around the window into the office and show them which rotary phone to use. They would stand there and gape, having never seen such a contraption. Lois would then show them that they used their finger to pick a number, twirl the dial, let it come back to rest and then repeat the procedure until the number was dialed. The kids were amazed and we all had a good time over this. However, a new touch-tone phone system in the office did away with this pleasure eventually. My own children agreed that I had now arrived in the 20th century. Recently a patient announced that she had found me on the Internet. How impressed are my children now?

An Attitude

One day a woman came into the waiting room as she had done several times before, glanced around and noted a black person waiting there. She marched up to the desk and informed my secretary that she would not be seated with any black person and stormed out. She immediately became an ex-patient of mine. It was a good thing that she left before I got wind of her attitude because she would have had to endure a piece of my mind, for which I undoubtedly would have wound up in trouble!

Mr. A.

One of my patients was difficult for several reasons. He had horrific asthma and was thoroughly non-compliant, he was a lawyer who didn't pay my bill without extensive dunning and he kept me on the telephone endlessly, at no charge. He, of course, would have been billing his time. One day, we were with another couple on the ferry to Nova Scotia from Bar Harbor, Maine when I went to the dining room. There he sat with his wife and his daughter. There was no way I could avoid them, and so I passed the time of day and went on. I heard his daughter say with great insight, "Daddy, he's trying to get away from you!" and, indeed, I was. The cruise passed uneventfully with regard to this patient and when we debarked I felt a sense of relief. That sense didn't last very long. We arrived at our lodgings, and after a drink on the lawn, went into the dining room. We were seated right next to my difficult patient and his family! As they were leaving his wife leaned over to me and said, cheerfully, "We're not going to tell you where we are staying tomorrow night." She knew. In the end he didn't have a problem during the night and we did not run across him again on our trip. I learned later that he and his wife had parted company, and eventually, he and I and I parted company as well.

An Airline Employee

One of my favorite patients was a lovely woman with a sharp wit. She worked for Delta Airlines. Her name was Dorothy Degan and she manned the Death Desk for the airline. This was where passengers were able to book flights quickly, change scheduled flights, etc, often because someone in their family was dead or dying. All day long, Dorothy said into the phone, "Dorothy Degan Delta Death Desk". How she managed to do this without losing her composure, I'm not sure, but I am sure she managed to help those in real need and was readily able to weed out the imposters.

Neighborliness

My associate was not given to angry outbursts. But one time, just after I had begun working in his office, I heard him raise his voice to a patient. I couldn't wait to see what that was all about. Then I heard him say, "Well, there's no sense paying me. Let your neighbor take care of you." It turned out of course, that the lady was not doing what he had advised her to do but, instead, had decided to treat herself the way her neighbor told her to. Over the years I had non-compliant patients, but they usually did not do what they should have on their own advice. I was never able to use his line, but I would have loved to! I know of one physician in Philadelphia who responds to these patients with a sign in his office: "The quality of your care depends upon who is the doctor, you or me!"

Giving the Baby Back

There was a young lady whom I had seen for many years who got married and was unable to conceive. So, she decided to adopt a baby. She seemed to know all about the baby girl who was brand new. It seems that the new Mama was adept at reading written material upside down and had followed along as the adoption people reviewed the child's chart before releasing her to her new mother. About two years later, she adopted a baby boy. She assured me that she knew all about the boy—same upside down reading technique. But, at around 6 months of age, the child began to thrive less and less well. Indeed, as I saw the family, I could tell that the child's development was very slow. When I asked the mother how she felt about this, she said that she and her husband were going to give the baby back! I had no idea that that could be done. About this time, the mother's treatment ended and I lost track of her and the children. Then, when the boy was about three years old, he appeared in my office with his mother, healthy, active, bright and obviously excellently developed. Luckily, before I had a chance to ask, Mama said that, yes, this was the same child that almost got given back. No one knew why his development had slowed or why he was now thriving, but we all agreed that it had been a close thing. I have often wondered if his mother ever told him about how close he came to being returned.

Global Amnesia

A lovely, very intelligent 60-65 year old patient of mine went with her husband to a business convention of his in another city. While he was out, at some point she lost her memory completely. She did not know who she was, where she was or any other pertinent information. Plainly she saw that she was in a hotel room, that she was married and that she was with her husband presumably since men's apparel items were nearby. So, she waited. Eventually, her husband returned and she realized that it was going to be impossible for her to keep her amnesia a secret. Of course, she very quickly wound up in the hospital with a diagnosis of global amnesia, the cause of which was never uncovered. Over several days she recovered completely (characteristic of this problem) and while I knew her she never had a recurrence or any other serious neurological problems. She did not relate the story in a humorous fashion however since it been such a frightening experience.

The Cop

One day a lady came into the treatment room from the waiting room, with what looked to me like a nervous smile. It seems that she had been followed all the way to the office by a police car, certain that the cop was on her tail for a reason. The more so when he turned into the parking lot right after she did. It never occurred to her that he might be coming to get his allergy shots.

Not even when he arrived in the waiting room after she did. I guess she was having a little episode of paranoia, but we ended up laughing about it and I introduced her to the officer who was a patient and a good friend of mine.

The Mellon Sisters

A physician who cared for many wealthy people and who sent us a lot of work used to encourage us to charge certain of his patients more than our normal fees. (We never did.) So one Saturday morning I was surprised by a phone call from him asking me to meet him at Westchester County Airport. We would be flying to Martha's Vineyard because "one of the Mellon sisters" had been stung by a jellyfish. Since I was not about to fly anywhere with him, I asked how long ago that had happened and was the woman still living. It had been several hours, maybe a day, and she was still with us. I pointed out that, in that case, he had no need of my services, nor did his patient. He was a bit disappointed I think because mainly he wanted company on the trip. But, he took it gracefully, knowing full well that I was right, and continued to send work my way, including, eventually, his wife.

The Parrot Lady

An older woman, about 75 years old came into the office one day because she needed to be tested for feathers. This seemed strange since she did not have a history of allergies. She explained that she was about to inherit a parrot which had been in the family for most of her life, and since it would live to be about 125 years old (and she probably would not) that meant she would be exposed to feathers for the rest of her life. She was a stately woman with a wonderful sense of humor, who, thankfully, tested negative to feathers. She left, happy in the knowledge that she would have a permanent companion without complications. The main problem then was to whom to leave the bird next, over which she and I had a hearty laugh!

R2D2

Several years ago I attended the national meeting of the American Academy of Allergy, Asthma and Immunology in San Antonio, Texas. Normally, I opted to attend sessions which were clinically oriented, but this day I went to a complex scientifically oriented meeting. Leukotrienes (chemicals involved in the immune inflammatory response) were just beginning to be studied and the subject would become important eventually in my daily practice. I noticed immediately that the physicians in attendance seemed quite young, and I realized that they were there so as not miss any new ideas which might crop up on their Board Certification exams. The presenter worked largely from slides, while the audience took notes copiously and furiously. Leukotrienes have names like leukotriene B, leukotriene C4, and leukotriene D4, and many of the slides were covered with corresponding notations. Suddenly, in the middle of the lecture, while everyone was jotting down his last remarks, the presenter flashed a picture of R2D2, a robot hero of Star Wars, onto the screen. This was labeled R2D2. I actually laughed when I saw virtually everyone, most of whom had grown up with Star Wars, immediately began to take notes on this hitherto unknown chemical! All soon realized what had happened and the room erupted in laughs and chuckles. The tense atmosphere lifted and I felt that the presenter had done just the right thing for his overzealous audience.

Her Last Breath

For several years I took care of a little girl with very severe, chronic asthma. It was in the days before all the new inhaled drugs that are able to control most cases so well were in use. She came to me with her mother every Tuesday, got her allergy shots and had her medicines revised if needed. One day, I was called to the hospital to see her after she had been admitted for breathing difficulties. Her pediatrician, the Chief of Pediatrics, arrived shortly after I did. Everything we could think of was done for this child. We were standing at her bedside and she was in obviously severe respiratory distress, when her pediatrician said, "Her next breath will be her last." So, we waited, and she breathed once more. We two doctors were beside ourselves with frustration over our inability to do more to help her. And then, she took another breath and another, still severely labored, but continuing to breathe. The medications were beginning to work. Eventually, she began to breathe more normally, and, several days later, she went home. To my knowledge, she never had such severe trouble again.

The postscript to the story: During July and August, every year, my office was closed on Thursday afternoons. This was posted from early April on every year. The girl's mother knew this quite well, her daughter having been a patient over several years. The first Thursday after the hospital incident, in July, the patient arrived with her mother, to find the office closed. Shortly thereafter, I was informed by letter that, henceforth, the little girl would be seeing another allergist, since I had had the audacity to change my office schedule without proper notice!

A Mid-day Drink

I had a friend who was a businessman in Manhattan during my training and thereafter. He was doing quite well for himself and knew how business got done in the City. I was totally unacquainted with the "business lunch". I had been out of training for just a matter of weeks when he said, "Let's do lunch." At the time, I was working in my soon to be partner's office in Manhattan several days a week. On Fridays, I worked in the morning, was off for several hours and then worked for two more hours in the afternoon. So, my friend and I arranged to have lunch on a Friday. Nothing would do but that I have a martini with my lunch. And, of course, another one. Lunch was lavish—he must have been paying!—and, so by the time I got back to the office, I felt just fine. Actually, I was horrified that I had to see patients after having those two drinks. I told my nurse, quite emphatically, that she was to keep an eye on me the rest of the day, which she did, following me everywhere and being present when I was seeing patients. Finally about an hour before the office closed, she burst out laughing. I asked what was so funny. She told me that she had never seen anybody being as careful about anything in her life as I had been during the afternoon, and, of course, by that time, there couldn't have been much alcohol in me anyway to cloud my judgment. I had to laugh, too, but never again did I see patients after having a drink.

Mistaken Identity

I began my internship at the same time as a tall, nice-looking fellow, Charles. For reasons which were unknown to me at the time and still are, people often confused the two of us. During training, which we did together, I got blamed for some revelry that I had not participated in, for instance. We both were quite used to this. We both began our medical practices in the same community. I often covered for another older doctor, for the first years I was in practice. One day in my second year of practice, I decided to take a weekend off. I really needed a break by then. On Saturday morning the older man called me, furious because I had not responded to a call from a patient of his. "I asked you to cover for me on the steps of the hospital yesterday!" No, I replied, he had got that wrong. There was a long silence, and then he said, "Well, whom did I ask?" "That would be Charles," I replied. And sure enough, it turned out to be another case of mistaken identity. All three of us laughed about it eventually, by the time the older man had cooled down. Charles was said to be the finest resident ever to train at St. Luke's-Roosevelt Hospital. He was our family's medical doctor for many years and saw our children after they reached adulthood. It was an honor to be confused with him!

Cat Allergy

Early on in our relationship it became clear that my wife was very sensitive to cats. So much so that she would sneeze and itch if someone visited us who had cats at home. Naturally, she is not fond of cats, but they seem attracted to her. One evening while visiting another home, she asked me where the cat was. I had not seen one, nor had she. However, a cat had just settled down behind her chair and Peggy was beginning to have symptoms.

As soon as the new cat treatment extract became available, Peggy began immunotherapy. It was easy to do since she was working regularly in the office by then. But, boy! Did we have to be careful giving her allergy shots. Large local reactions and occasional hives guided her dosages. Soon, she began to tolerate cats much better, and eventually became "immune" to the exposure. After about 5 years of treatment, the shots were discontinued and she continues to do well these many years later. She still avoids cats as much as possible, the children have gotten rid of their cats and the people we visit try to keep her exposure to their cats to a minimum. The antihistamines are always in readiness.

Mrs. Purse

On the way home from the office, my wife, carrying the office envelope and her purse, was mugged at knife point. We had often worried that this would happen in the City, but no, it took place at high noon on the main road into White Plains. She knew there was trouble when she saw a man going in the opposite direction on foot, turn around, cross the street and begin to follow her. She did not turn into the entrance to the residential park where we lived and where she probably would not have been seen, but instead continued on down the main sidewalk. The mugger soon displayed a large knife and grabbed her purse. (The office envelope had more money in it.) She screamed, the mugging was witnessed from an apartment nearby where the observers dialed 911. A man in a van who also saw it, managed to corner the mugger up against a wall with his truck. Luckily for him, he did not injure the perp, who then threw the knife down a storm drain. The police arrived, arrested the mugger and retrieved the knife. About then a colleague came upon the scene in his well-known white Cadillac, and was horrified to see Peggy sitting in the back of the squad car. He stopped to see what that was all about. Eventually, Peggy wound up at the police station where I eventually found her.

When the case came to the grand jury, Peggy was on hand. One of our best friends was senior assistant DA in Westchester. He called Peggy into his office to await her turn in court. He also told the young DA on the case, to be sure not to make any mistakes. When she was called, our friend went into the jury room as well, onto the balcony. When the young DA spotted his boss, he became so flustered that he began his questioning of my wife by saying, "Now then, Mrs. Purse . . ." A slightly embarrassing but humorous error in the courtroom. The mugger eventually served over two years in jail. This was his first and only offence on record. We hope it was a lesson well learned.

The Crossing Guard

For several years, a neighbor rode with me on Monday mornings into Manhattan. We usually took the same route which included getting to Martin Luther King Jr. Boulevard in Harlem on the cross street at 136th

Street. At that corner, there was always the same crossing guard when we arrived. The first time we saw her it was raining and she was wearing a full length bright yellow raincoat and rain hat. She looked for all the world like a huge banana! Whenever we saw her in this outfit we always had a laugh. Eventually, she began to notice us on our regular schedule and we would all wave at each other. Then we began to stop and chat if she was not busy shepherding children across the busy intersection. We never learned each others' names, but our association put a bright spot in our Monday morning trip to work even if it was raining.

My Son George

One day a lovely lady came to see me. After we were face to face across my desk, she remarked that she knew my son George. Being in practice in my hometown where my father had been quite well known, I was used to people saying to me that they knew my father. I guess I looked a little bewildered as we proceeded with the interview. At the end, I commented about my initial reaction since I usually heard a different remark. It turned out that this lady was my George's nursery school teacher, and that she had not known my father. We both had a good laugh over this and would comment on it from time to time over the years while she was a patient.

The Subway to Queens

For about two years, I would take the subway to Grand Central Station and the train to Scarsdale to pick up my car and drive home. This happened on Wednesdays when I would leave the office at about 5:30 PM. One night, after I got on the subway, I realized that the trip was taking far too long even though we were speeding along, and that there were no stations. So, I guessed that I had gotten on the train to Queens and was traveling under the East River. This added at least 40 minutes to my trip and did not make me happy. I thought no more about it other than to be a little annoyed at myself, when, the following week I did the exact same thing. By now I am wondering what is going on in my head, and I resolved not to make this mistake again, and I never did. My wife was thoroughly amused at the time, and it does seem amusing to me now.

The Smithsonian

There was an allergist in a neighboring town who was a very old man. He still continued to see patients—they would bring their treatment solutions from the kitchen refrigerator upstairs to his bedroom where he would administer the shots. Eventually, a family member asked me if I would be willing to see his remaining patients and I readily agreed. (Some were still patients by the time I retired!) When he died, his daughter was in a quandary about what to do with his 1929 style office which had long been unused. Inspired, she called the Smithsonian Institution to ask if they had need of such an office. To her utter surprise, they sent a team to inspect the office and, even more surprising, took the whole office, lock, stock and stethoscope to be set up as an exhibit in Washington. To my knowledge, it remains there to this day.

His Nickname

I was seeing a young man once whose mother insisted that I call him by his nickname. It was "John". His given name was, of course, "Jack". Jack was written on his chart and so I often called him Jack before I got my brain around his nickname being John. After his mother reprimanded me for doing this several times, I couldn't help but explain to her that her son was the only person in the English speaking world to be nicknamed John and that she would just have to be patient with me. I have wondered what Jack's nickname became after he got off to school and out of the house.

A Cancellation

A matter of days after I opened my office, practicing internal medicine and allergy (I later concentrated in allergy) I was sitting at my desk within earshot of the secretary with nothing to do. This secretary had worked for the doctor from whom I was renting part of an office for many years. When I heard her say that my appointment book was full, I bounded out of my office to confront her. It took me a moment to grasp the scene. There she was thumbing rapidly through my nearly empty appointment book with the telephone receiver lying next to the book on the desktop.

Suddenly, she stopped turning pages, glanced at the current day's page and, picking up the receiver, announced that she had discovered a cancellation that very afternoon. The patient took the appointment. My secretary quietly closed the book and looked up at me with an angelic if slightly smug smile. What fun it was to be around a person who really knew the ropes!

A Stuffy Nose

The husband of a couple we occasionally saw socially appeared in my New York office complaining of a stuffy nose. It was very early in my career. I knew about stuffy noses, but then he informed me that this only happened when he was sexually aroused. This I was not sure about and so after he left having had a few of the usual preliminary skin tests, I ran to the books. The answer was quite simple. There is erectile-type tissue in the nose and when it engorges with blood it can actually produce nasal stuffiness. (This is why stuffiness can be a side effect of the ED drugs.) So, of course this was not allergic at all and was nicely handled with a nasal decongestant used before sex. Made me feel rather clever. Of course, I never mentioned the patient's condition to anyone remotely connected to my social life.

MOMA

A little, elderly, very wealthy lady bustled into my office one day in high dudgeon. This by itself was alarming because she was so petite and always sweet-natured. I asked what was up and she replied that she had just come from the Metropolitan Museum of Modern Art. She spotted a featured painting which consisted of a large, pure white square with the tiniest of red dots in the center. This, she decided, was not art, modern or otherwise, and that therefore she would no longer be gifting the Museum. At a loss as to what to say, I suggested that maybe later she would change her mind, but she was having none of it. I didn't inquire about her decision at later visits since she had been so upset by it in the first place and I never got to the Museum to see the offending painting.

Occupational Hazards

One of my favorite patients was a very attractive widow in her early eighties, looking as if she might be 60-65. She was quite well off and kept very active. I had three problems with her, however. She kept following me around the office and, on occasion, would simply walk right into my office while I was seeing another patient. My reaction when this would happen was amusing, mainly to the other patient. Another problem was over her bill. She complained to me bitterly one day about my fee. It was the Medicare allowed fee, about $35.00 less than it would have been otherwise. She had Medicare and all kinds of insurance supplementals. The same lady however, thought nothing of paying her ophthalmologist $8000.00 (!) more than the Medicare approved fee for cataract surgery. Not only was it illegal for the eye doctor to charge such an amount, but, it was illegal for the patient to pay it. When I asked if she was going to report the doctor she took issue with this idea saying that she loved the woman (her eye doctor) so much that she would never object to her bill. I'm afraid that I then took issue with her complaint about my bill. Not long after, she called from Florida to insist that I write a letter indicating that it was medically necessary for her to stay there for a longer period of time. I carefully explained that, since I had not seen her before she left and that no indication of any sort for doing this was recorded in her chart, it would be unethical at least and probably illegal if I wrote such a letter and the insurance company found that there was no record of this necessity in her chart. Unfortunately this did not discourage her from continuing as my patient or from following me around the office.

Drink Coaster?

Whenever it became necessary to identify the molds present in someone's home, mold plates (basically Petri dishes) were obtained, exposed around the house, then re-covered and sent off to the company lab for identification of what grew on them. We had a good laugh with one patient over the use of the exposed mold plates. It seemed that his brother-in-law (of all people) was enjoying a drink at the house and decided that the mold plate on the table in the living room was a coaster for his drink. It was some time before my patient noticed the problem. He corrected his guest and then continued to keep the plate exposed. He carefully marked it and noted the problem to us. Molds were identified in that room, but we did wonder if this was an accurate discovery!

The Condom Lady

There was a very attractive lady whom I had gotten to know because she came to the White Plains office frequently with her daughter. Eventually, the young girl, equally pretty, went off to college and was discharged from care. Several years later, the mother arrived in my office in New York. She was there she said because she had a little problem, allergic in nature, which came up after she began dating a man about whom she was becoming quite serious. She said that if they become intimate, with the AIDS problem, she wanted to be able to protect herself. Unfortunately, she was allergic to latex. I naturally advised her about "sheep skin" condoms, but with the caveat that the AIDS virus might not be stopped by these. She immediately began to smile when she realized what I had to say next, that her friend would have to use a latex condom under the natural one. At that point we were both chuckling. But then we had a really good laugh when she asked what would happen if he was allergic to latex as well. The idea of using three condoms at one time struck both of us as hysterically funny, but she seemed satisfied with the consultation.

About a year later, while I was standing on the buffet line at a hospital medical center annual ball, I felt a tap on my shoulder. When I turned around, there was my patient, on the arm of one of the leading physicians in town. Over the years, he had sent me many patients and I had cared for some of his family members. I knew he had been widowed and was remarried. When I saw who my patient had been referring to at our consultation, I was even more amused. Had I known, I could have assured her that she had no need to worry about her new gentleman friend. As it was, the two of us greeted each other without going into gales of laughter. I have wondered if she ever told her new husband about our consultation. My wife, of course, knew both people involved and she was privy to the whole funny story.

Flu Shots

Once again it was the flu season. A group of friends spent a long weekend every year at one friend's beach house. We called it "The Adult Weekend". One of the wives in the group, who was a patient of mine, had already had her flu shot in my office. I knew that all the others thought themselves too busy to take time for the shot. So, I brought along vaccine and needles in a brown paper bag. As soon as everyone had arrived and we were having the first drink of the day, I announced that they should all line up for their flu shots. Such a commotion! Well, they all did line up and had their flu shots except, of course, my patient who expressed herself thus, "Well, Goddammit, if I had known I could have gotten a free shot I never would have had one in your office." Everyone knew that she did not spend any money out of pocket coming to see me professionally, but that did not keep her from railing on about it to the accompaniment of howls of laughter!

The Affair

Though young, he was one of the leading doctors in my community. He was a well known prima donna, as are many doctors, barely noticing my presence at conferences and meetings. He was married to a colleague of mine who was much involved in the politics of medicine. (Women doctors married to successful men, often other doctors, are able to run their practices without much attention to what income they earn. The reverse is true also, of course.) At a luncheon meeting in another town, I noted a very attractive woman pass by our table. I was seated so that I could see into the rest of the restaurant. Soon, I saw my colleague's husband circle around the room and come up behind my chair. He whispered into my ear not to tell his wife that I had seen him here. The other people at the table looked at him curiously as he left, but the only note that was made of it was that his wife was not at our meeting as she would normally be. From then on, this physician greeted me warmly whenever he saw me, which I found greatly amusing though I remained thoroughly annoyed that I was expected to keep his secret. Just before I sold my practice, I joked to my wife at breakfast that, if the offer I was expecting was not satisfactory, I should perhaps suggest to the philanderer that he buy my practice for his wife. My wife was scandalized to be sure but we both found the idea amusing.

I'm a Surgeon!

Another example of high regard for one's self occurred one night when I was on my way home from a social occasion, which involved a young physician whom I had not seen before or since. I was driving over the Hutchinson River Parkway when I noted what looked to be an accident on the roadway below. I pulled to the side of the road, about to have a look down below when another car with MD plates pulled up behind me. The occupant of this car rushed to have a look too, nearly knocking me over and then sprang down the bridge embankment all the time yelling, "I'm a surgeon, I'm a surgeon!" With rescue vehicles arriving and such an enthusiastic doctor on the scene, I felt my presence was not necessary. So, I continued on my way discussing with my wife the impertinent young man, who, from my license plates knew that I was also a physician. How he knew I was most assuredly not a surgeon I do not know.

The Food Challenge

This is another hard to believe story, but true. A mother brought her early-teen aged son in because he had been diagnosed as allergic to wheat. He did have allergic symptoms whenever he ate food containing wheat. His mother decided that he was merely faking the problem and that he was not allergic to wheat at all. We arranged to do a double-blind wheat challenge, very carefully. It became apparent quickly that the boy was allergic to wheat and that a really severe enough reaction might be fatal. And so, the mother and her son were educated extensively on how they should manage his diet. Luckily, this was a very smart kid who was interested in staying out of allergic trouble. He had none, but about a year later he showed up again with his mother, who by this time had grown tired of trying to keep wheat out of his diet. She insisted that he be retested. This time, we used a small amount of wheat to test him and he immediately developed symptoms. My main concern now was the boy so the discussion of his diet involved mainly him. He was quite happy to follow a wheat-free diet and not take any chances. His mother was not happy, but eventually he went off to college, quite able to manage what his mother had been so unwilling to do for him.

Marie

Since I was usually able to spend a fair amount of time with my patients, I came to know some of them quite well and often we became good friends. They would tell me stories about their own lives. Some are worthy of repeating.

Marie has been a patient and then a good friend of mine for many years. She is now a retired schoolteacher, linguist and world traveler. At one time airport bombings were all the rage. She and a friend arrived at Leonardo da Vinci airport in Rome one day at Christmastime. As they were standing on the passport inspection line, an airport employee said that another line was opening up in a different location if they were interested in speeding up their arrival in Italy. So they moved away from where they had been standing, where, almost immediately, a terrorist bomb went off, killing many. Marie and her companion dove under a banquette near a window where they stayed for several hours. Then, they were put on a bus, to sit some more. Eventually, military people boarded and examined everyone and everything on the bus. Finally, passport checks having been forgotten, their bus was allowed to depart for downtown Rome and thence to their hotel. Marie was always somewhat over-concerned for her health, but this episode did not deter her in the least from traveling. I kid her to this day about how close she came to disaster, but that she had managed to survive the airport attack even without my reassurances.

Because of her health concerns, I sent Marie to one of the finest internal medicine specialists in New York City. He had been a college and medical school classmate of mine and was in the enviable position of being able to limit the size of his practice. I practically begged him to see Marie as I had done with a few other patients. Years later at our college 50th reunion, I asked him to remember me to the patients I had sent him whom he was still seeing. He said, "I can't." Taken aback, I wondered why. He said that then he would have to sit and listen to them explain how wonderful Dr. Hermance was. Indeed, a fine compliment from a fine physician.

The Cardinal's Sister

Miss L was, as she often said, an "unplucked rose", which amused me no end. She came from a family of high achievers, a Cardinal of the Church, a famous thoracic surgeon and a judge among others. She functioned as the hostess for her brother the Cardinal, in the Midwest, so she was frequently off on another trip to make arrangements for or to travel with her brother. Two stories she told me stand out.

Miss L. was accompanying her brother the Cardinal and his valet on a trip by air. At the airport, she went through the metal detector first and the valet came next, both without trouble. However, when His Eminence passed through the gate, all the bells and whistles went off. He emptied his pockets, took off his watch, etc. and still the metal detector went off. This took several passes thru the machine before the valet suddenly started pawing through the Cardinal's clothes until he found the Miraculous Medal he had pinned to his undershirt that morning. After it was removed the Cardinal was, quite miraculously, able to pass the metal detector test.

Her best story however, involved a birthday party she was hosting for her brother, an Archbishop then, at the Chancellery. After the party was in full swing for awhile, finding that the Archbishop had not appeared, everyone sat down to dinner. About midway through the meal, the Bishop appeared, thanked everyone for coming and left. In the morning, early, Miss L's bedside phone rang. She told me that she immediately suspected that it would be her brother. It was and he wanted to know if she had heard the morning news. She had not, but soon did, and learned that her brother had been elevated to Cardinal. The Papal Nuncio, who traditionally delivers this news, had called just before the birthday party to tell Miss L.'s brother, in Latin, the news. The Cardinal asked him to please repeat the message in Italian since he understood so little Latin! The Nuncio also asked him not to tell anyone until he had heard it on the news. The Bishop knew he would not be able to hide his pleasure at the news during the party and so he had elected not to spend much time there. Miss L.'s suspicion was right on though. Indeed her brother was now a Cardinal of the Church.

Car Calls

After I began to practice allergy and immunology exclusively, I stopped making house calls for the most part. However, I did wind up making "car calls". One patient was a well-known Judge. He was a faithful patient for many years, until he became unable to come into the office. He did tool around New York in a big black limousine however, and, about every two weeks during office hours, he would call to say that he would be parked at the curb downstairs so that I could go down and give him his allergy shots. I was happy to perform this service for him, but, I must say, the first time felt a little weird to me. There I was walking from my building to his limo, balancing my paraphernalia, and being ushered into the interior of the car. The Judge already had his sleeves rolled up for his injections. We had an office visit just as we would have had in the office. I gave him his shots and cheerfully went back upstairs and back to work. I remember that the limo stayed parked for the requisite 20 minutes after the injections. I wondered how to explain my biweekly limo rides, but, since there wasn't any riding, there was not much for me to tell.

Another long time patient and a favorite one eventually became too ill with neurological disease to come into the White Plains office. Her husband reluctantly asked what arrangements could be made for her treatments. Since he drove her regularly to the office anyway, I suggested that his wife could have her shots without getting out of the car. This worked very well, and was still going on when I retired. The young doctor who worked for me was happy to continue this arrangement, which made one less problem for me to deal with.

"Don't Tell Me about It!"

Like many allergists, I often saw patients once every three months and provided them with medication (extracts) for other medical people to administer in a medical setting. I was quite strict about who was giving the shots as well as the visit to my office, which was required. A young student who had been a patient for several years eventually went to college. Naturally, I assumed that he was receiving his injections in the college health facility. In reality, his roommate was administering them! Unintentionally or not, he told me about this arrangement. I called his mother. Her response was: "I don't want to know about it." Well, I certainly didn't either and told the young man, after carefully explaining the reasons why he shouldn't be doing that, "Don't tell me about it!" He survived college and his allergy shots, thankfully.

Another patient who went on to college arranged with a group of his new friends to all go together to an allergist in town to get their shots. Easier and more fun I suppose than using the college health service.

My Cousin's Coach

A famous football player and would-be politician arrived in the office one day. As we were chatting, I discovered that he had coached the Army football team at one time. My cousin, the Lt. Colonel, had been a football player at The Point and indeed had been coached by my patient, who remembered him as the finest center that he had ever worked with. Just another example of a small world. (On my mother's side of the family, the Blake Family considered the Lt. C and the MD to be outstanding members of the tribe!)

A Romanian Husband

One of my favorite patients is a school teacher in New York City, an energetic lady with a wonderful sense of humor. While she was in treatment, she married a man from Romania, long a resident of the States, but whose family was still in Europe. One day I asked her how she managed to communicate with her mother-in-law when she went to visit her husband's family. It was quite simple, she explained. She had learned forty words in Romanian which could be used to describe her husband in the most complimentary terms and she used them freely whenever his mother brought up the subject of him or his family. Eventually, this couple adopted two beautiful girls from his native country, both of whom have grown into lovely, accomplished young women. I know this because their pictures and an update come to me every year from the family.

Three Generations

As I have mentioned earlier, one of the most appealing attractions of my specialty is the continuity of care which can be afforded patients. It was my privilege to know many people for many years and to watch whole families grow up. As I started in practice, I cared for a diamond merchant who had asthma. Luckily, he was very compliant, and so, even though he still had asthma, he continued to be a patient whose problem was well controlled when I retired 31 years later! I even knew that his daughter's marriage had failed but that he had kept his ex-son-in-law in the business with him and considered him to be an excellent asset to the business.

Early on I also began seeing a woman who was also a social friend of ours. Her children were very young and very allergic. Eventually, they all became patients. And, I remember well the day that her son brought his oldest son in for treatment, the first third generation patient I saw. Eventually, his wife and his three children became patients—all except one were highly allergic, his daughter having only a little problem now and then. Eventually there were several multigenerational patients in the practice, a very rewarding experience for any doctor.

Dr. P

Dr. P. was the leading allergist in Georgia and perhaps in the South when I first began my practice. One day, a lovely looking slightly older lady with a southern accent arrived in my office for a second opinion consultation. Why she picked me is still a mystery, but I was alarmed when she handed me a three page single-spaced typewritten letter she had received as Dr. P.'s report to her. She told me not to bother with the first two pages but to read the last line of the report. It said, "Mrs. Z, you are the kind of patient who, when she walks in the front door, the doctor wants to run out of the back door!"

I was unsure whether to laugh or cry, but Mrs. Z turned out to be a very easy patient to deal with who was satisfied with my care. Several years later, I had dinner with Dr. P. a tall handsome southern gentleman. I managed not to tell on Mrs. Z. and to this day I have no idea what caused the good doctor to pen the "offending" line.

A Height-challenged Boy

After I had been seeing a young man for some time, his mother, slightly round and very short, asked if I would speak to her in my office about a problem with her son. I did so, and during the consultation, I could tell that she was very upset about how short her son was. The more she talked the more I wondered about her husband, and so I finally asked as carefully as I could about how tall the boy's father was. Well, he was 5'2". Then, again as gently as I could, I explained that her son was not likely to be very tall, but would probably be taller than she and his father, that boys grew until they were in late teens and even early twenties. We discussed human growth hormone which was not in wide use then for height problems in children.

He was an excellent boy, smart, popular by all accounts, extremely outgoing and generally nice to have around. I knew he would find the right girl eventually and that height differences among the sexes were causing fewer problems than in the past. The last time I saw him, he was finished with college and stopped in the office for a social visit. It was plain then that he would be successful in his life despite his height and that he was at ease with his stature (about 5'5" to 5'7", I guessed). He had not had any problem dating, often girls taller than he.

Ill Advised Therapies

Once, in his earlier years, my partner was seeing a patient who was apparently allergic to newspaper print. His suggestion was for the man to dry the paper out thoroughly before reading it. He was to do this by heating it in the oven. You can guess the result!

On rounds one day I came across a young child with severe eczema. It has been said that eczema is an itch in search of a rash. Repeated scratching trauma to the skin results in infection and the chronically abnormal skin of eczema. This child was tied down on his bed by his arms and feet. He certainly couldn't scratch, but it seemed to me to be a particularly awful form of torture.

A similar thought crossed my mind, when, again on rounds, I came across a man with the most awful case of poison ivy I had ever seen. This, I thought must be the reason for his hospitalization, but, it was not. He had been given the skin disease (contact allergy) on purpose as a counterirritant for his cardiac-related chest pain. Thankfully we have progressed a bit beyond these treatments today.

A Long Island Wedding

My secretary invited us to her wedding. It was held in a well-known wedding establishment on Long Island. The bride wore white—she was lovely, but, her mother wore gold lame and stole the show! I sported a yellow yarmulke. We adjourned to the reception hall which was immense and featured a real stage with an orchestra below. Across the stage was the table for the large wedding party. The servers wore yellow gloves. We were having a wonderful time, when suddenly, there was a terrible crash. I looked toward the stage and there I saw a row of people sitting, sans table. The table had fallen off the stage into the orchestra. All was set well so fast that some people missed the whole thing I think, and no one was hurt. The reception went on as if nothing had happened and a good time was had by all.

Parallel Lines

During the Nixon administration, price fixing was in effect for a period of time. The fee for a regular office visit at that time was $10.00. Physicians were among the last group to be decontrolled, but at one point we were told we could raise our fee 2.5 % to $10.25. The accountant advised us to do so and from then on the office was awash in quarters. People would pay their bills by check or cash and, of course, bookkeeping for them was easier if they just handed over a quarter. For a time thereafter, we found quarters in some very odd places.

Later, we were told that we could raise fees again on the basis of our current fees. Many doctors were unhappy that they had not bothered to raise their fees the first time. In any case, the fee became $11.00 for an office visit. At the very next billing, the calls began to come in. What did the quotation marks on the bills mean? Why were there parallel lines after the dates of office visits? The office staff had fun explaining these mysteries to the patients who, for the most part, accepted them with good humor.

Thoughtful Thieves

On my way to work along 55th Street, I came into contact with another man, sort of a brush up against. A short distance away there was a receptacle for trash. Lying there on the edge was my date book which had lately been residing in the breast pocket of my open suit jacket. Astounded that I had not noticed anything unusual, I was even more amazed at finding my book. I have ever after thought of the other man as "the considerate pickpocket"!

Again near Central Park a man approached and demanded my money. Like an idiot, I took out my wallet, gave about half of the money in it to the thief, announcing that I needed the rest for my day's expenses. The thief was brandishing a tiny pocket knife at me. Then he noticed the ring I wore and demanded that, exhorting me not to yell. I immediately began to shout but, by the time I had really made any noise the man was gone with about $40.00 of mine but no wallet or ring. Another considerate (?) thief.

The Cadillac

I once owned a beautiful Cadillac, calypso green in color. Usually, on my way to the office, I drove down through the middle of Harlem to the north entrance of Central Park. While the car was brand new, I pulled up to a stop light on Martin Luther King, Jr. Boulevard. Another car came up next to me. The driver, a black man, in a very nice car of his own, rolled down his window indicating that I should do likewise. I did so and we sat through a couple of light changes while he explained that my car may have been the most beautiful car he had ever seen. We both drove off with smiles and I still chuckle when I remember the scene.

And You a Doctor!

In a different car on a dark and stormy night, as Snoopy would say, I was negotiating the complicated exit from the Cross Bronx Expressway to the Bronx River Parkway, northbound. I did this many times before and after, but on this night I gently bumped the car in front of me. It was clear that the other driver, whose car was full of people, wanted to discuss this with me and so we rolled a short distance into an unused, unlit gas station. We both peered at our cars to inspect the damage. Luckily, there was none to either car. He, of course noted my MD license plate. As he stalked off to his car (from which I expected to be attacked any minute) he said, clearly disgusted, "And you a doctor!" Uncharacteristically, I kept my mouth shut and was able to drive off unharmed. By the time I got home, I thought the whole thing was humorous. I didn't at the time though, and my wife has never thought so. We usually comment on the event when we travel that intersection now.

The Chihuahua

A tiny elderly lady never arrived in my office in Manhattan without her cloth tote bag. It was quite large. She never made any fuss over it, just placed it on the floor beside her chair while she received her injections. One day I got a glimpse of the bag's contents and discovered a Chihuahua inside. Of course, animals of any kind were not allowed in the office, but, before I said anything, I inquired of my partner if he knew about this. Of course, he had known about it for years and was surprised to learn that this was a new finding for me. He noted that this was one of his longest-term patients and he could not (would not?) bring himself to say anything to her. Neither did I, and so she and I continued to get along just fine. I know we had a great relationship. At the time the movie "I Am Curious Yellow" appeared in a theater on 57th Street and there were always long lines outside the movie house to see this "pornographic" film. One day my little lady, who passed the theater on her way to the office, announced to me that, "If all those people had any sense they would all be home 'doing it' instead of standing on that line!" Made my day.

Billy

I have been called by many names, among them, Bill, Billy, Billy H., William, Willie, Hermie, and Doc. The names that people used were determined by when we were best acquainted. So, if I heard myself referred to as Billy, it was likely to by someone I had gone to elementary school with. One of my patients was a friend of mine from kindergarten through high school. He was the coach for two of my boys who were baseball players. He is a great big, lovely man and often his visits to the office would turn into reminiscing if we had the time. In the waiting room, whenever he would see someone he had not noticed on prior visits, he would launch into stories about Billy. His favorite one revolved around the fact that I was not an athlete and when teams were being made up during gym, or even just casually, Billy was always picked last. (And usually sent out to play right field.) My patients all thought this was very funny and responded to him and to me with comments about how lucky it was that I was not their surgeon, and the like.

The International Doctor

The first medical problem that my grandson developed while he and his family were living in Lagos, Nigeria was malaria. Despite extensive precautions and preventive medicines, he was diagnosed at the tender age of 12 months. So, one day I found myself talking by phone with the Chief Medical Officer of Mobil Oil. Of course, I had studied the disease in school but I had never seen a case. When I heard about Benjamin, I hit the books fast and soon found myself consulting with said medical officer holding a book in one hand and the phone in the other. Benjamin recovered with the correct medicines and then was well until he developed a variant of tuberculosis in the lymph nodes in his neck. Same doctor, same scenario, but this time Benjamin's mother had to bring him to us in New York. (Mobil wanted to send mother and son to London for treatment, but my daughter-in-law saw to it, in no uncertain terms, that they would be going to New York City!) My colleagues in White Plains were simply terrific about caring for Benjamin. Eventually, despite massive drug treatment facilitated by some dedicated pharmacists in town, he wound up having surgery at New York Medical College where I was an adjunct professor. No complications ensued. His father was transferred to Dallas, TX soon thereafter where Benjamin's problem recurred. He was operated on again, again without complications or significant scarring. This time the problem was eliminated. We often chuckle at Benjamin's medical history which he will have to write down with every visit to a new doctor, including as it does two very third-world medical problems.

My last foray into international doctoring came when Benjamin's sister, Meghan, developed intestinal amebiasis and salmonellosis at the same time. By now the family was in Doha, Qatar. Once again, she was treated successfully but not before she became a very sick little girl. Her treatment continued and was completed in the States. Scary moments for the family given that the patients were so far from our American medical system. A good thing was that the Emir's son was Meghan's friend and classmate at the American School and the medical staff assumed that she was "under the protection of the Emir". She received the very best "boutique" medical and nursing care!

Bora Bora

One of my patients was a very wealthy woman who was allergic to her dog. She was receiving treatments for this, and doing fairly well. One day she announced to me that she always had trouble in the apartment in Manhattan and almost always at her country house, but that she never had trouble in the house on Bora, Bora. "Bora, Bora?" I exclaimed incredulously. I really felt like laughing out loud, but I managed to keep my face on and wondered if she had her dog with her in Bora Bora. Well, of course, she did not take her dog there and so, of course, she had no allergies while on the island. One of the reasons that this struck me so funny was that my partner, a world traveler, had never been to Bora Bora and I knew that he would not be able to keep from asking her all about the place.

Grass Pollen Allergy

When I was about 12 years old, earning my living by mowing lawns, I developed a severe allergy to grass pollen. This made spring a miserable time for me. Antihistamines and air conditioning were virtually unheard of in my circle, and so I was not happy. During college I used Pyribenzamine to control symptoms, but it made me groggy and so I supplemented this medicine with NoDoz to get through the spring semester. This continued unabated until service in Springfield, Missouri. I had two years free from symptoms because, I guess, the pollen there was sufficiently different so that my immune system didn't recognize it. Finally, when I started practice, my partner would give me shots, carefully. I tested highly positive and so, while we liked to get patients up to doses of 10,000 to 20,000 units, the highest I ever got after three years was 350 units. Despite this I had complete resolution of my symptoms. Now, some 40 years later, I am once again experiencing mild spring hayfever. The non-sedating antihistamines work wonderfully well, but there are times when I have to retreat to an air conditioned space for relief.

The Non-compliant Crowd

One of the most difficult problems in medicine is non-compliance by patients with their doctor's orders. Two cases in particular stand out for me.

A lady in the New York office was a nurse at a hospital in Manhattan. She had terrible asthma. Every few weeks she would show up in the office in severe trouble. She would get emergency treatment and then a plan for her long term care. She always required oral cortisone for treatment in high, decreasing daily doses. I think she never missed a day at work even when in severe distress. She lived alone. I knew she stopped taking her meds as soon as she felt better, but I couldn't see how she benefited from this (secondary gain). Finally, I called her daughter about this problem. She noted that she knew her mother was non-compliant, that she had tried to help with the problem to no avail. And so, the woman's cycle of wellness and profound distress continued until I retired. I hope her next doctor had better luck with her.

On the other hand, there was a woman in the White Plains office who had the same pattern of non-compliance. Sometimes it was difficult getting her out of trouble with her asthma. One day I decided to try to get to the bottom of this problem with her. To my surprise when I questioned her about it, she readily noted that the only attention she got from her husband was when she began to have severe breathing problems. So, this lady actually had something to gain from not using her medicines correctly and thereby getting her husband to notice her!

Names

I have had two patients by the name of Elspath a name I had not heard before. I saw a young Spanish woman whose name was Eufrasia, spelled slightly differently than my mother's name, Euphrasia.

I assumed of course when Ms. Musumecci told me she was getting married that she might like her new name better. That was until she told me that she was going to marry Mr. Schiavoni. We laughed over that and then again several years later when she told me that she really had wanted an hyphenated name, she being a young business woman. She regrettably had to reconsider this desire after her wedding.

I have seen two patients with the last name Loony. One was, one wasn't. My partner's friend had a normal name, Harry and an astonishing, not to say off-putting, last name. When they met while traveling in Europe, Harry noted that he had changed his name legally. My partner was nonplussed when his friend told him his new, first name, was Howard. His last name remained unchanged.

Seen outside the office, some patients are difficult to attach a name to. My partner met a young patient of ours in Heathrow airport. (This young man was the only person I ever cared for who refused to have his injection site cleaned with alcohol.) Half way across the Atlantic Ocean my partner finally remembered his name.

There was the patient whose name was Jack and whose mother insisted he be called by his nickname-John!

And then there was Mrs. J., an operatic voice teacher who came to the New York office and, rarely, to the White Plains office where my wife worked for many years. At the Ritz hotel in Barcelona, in the elegant dining room there, sparsely populated this evening, I spotted Mrs. J. and her husband. I asked el mesero in Spanish, what their name might be, since I couldn't remember no matter how I racked my brain. No deal—not allowed to give out guest's names. Then I asked my wife who said, "I work in the White Plains office. I cannot be expected to know the names of New York City patients." So, there we sat, until quite some time later my wife said, "That will be Mrs. J." I knew she had it right and went over to their table and was greeted with hugs and kisses and much chatter. Los meseros looked on which I was glad to see.

And, while I was in the service, Ms. Klahn married Dr. Klan becoming Mrs. Klahn-Klahn.

My wife's OB-GYN doctor in Springfield, MO, was Dr. M.D. Bonebrake, M.D. Why he wasn't an orthopedist, despite the spelling, none of us could figure out.

Then, of course, when Dr. Doctor showed up at my training hospital, the emergency in-house call had to be changed from "Doctor, Doctor" to "Doctor Quick".

Gingersnaps

A young man about 16 years old came to the office, referred from a nearby hospital emergency room. He had been there several days previously when he was treated for acute anaphylactic shock. He was employed at the pool at a local country club for the summer. In the past, he had had acute allergic reactions to ginger and was careful to avoid any foods in which ginger appeared to be an ingredient. His reaction this time began shortly after eating lunch supplied by the country club. He had not sustained a bee sting and so the possibilities for trouble seemed related to his lunch. He had had a hamburger which he remembered as being excellent along with some other fixings. He had had all of these things before with no problem. We asked him to have the club chef describe the contents of the hamburger. The chef allowed as how he always put some finely crumbled gingersnaps into his ground round when making hamburger patties. I don't think my young patient's summer was ruined, but he was careful thereafter to eat meals that he brought from home!

Marrying Harry

Over the years I saw many clergy persons. One of my favorites was a nun who was quite young when she first became a patient in the White Plains office. One day, after her shots, she said that she was glad not to have had to wait long to be seen because she had to hurry back to the convent so as not to miss the vote. The vote was to decide whether or not to shorten by a very small amount the skirts of the habit her order wore. I wondered whether or not her side (to shorten) would win and she replied, "No, all those girls who should have married Harry 40 years ago will vote against it!" And right she was, the habits stayed long.

Several years later, the New York office, my secretary came into my office to say that there was a pleasant looking woman wearing a colorful summer dress standing at the front desk. She said that the woman claimed to be a nun. I knew in an instant who it would be, and sure enough, there stood my nun grinning from ear to ear. I allowed as how her side, it seemed, had finally won and we had a good laugh over Harry before we settled down to discuss her medical business.

Check Bouncing

Especially in the New York City office many patients were young, professional women. One day, I heard my secretary discussing a check from one of these ladies which had bounced. I knew she had bounced another check in the past, so I was intrigued by the conversation. The patient carefully explained that on the first of the month she always paid all her bills and that a check rarely bounced at the same business two months in row. Our suggestion was that for the foreseeable future she should make sure to pay our bill first, a day before the other bills in the hope that our check would reach the bank while there was still some money in her account. I guess she did—we had no further problem with her payments.

Penicillin Allergy

Reactions to penicillin can be fatal, often swiftly so. A case in point was a nurse I saw after she had had a near fatal reaction. She knew she was highly allergic to the drug so much so that she would arrange to be away from her nursing station if penicillin was being readied for a patient. Her young son was given penicillin to take and when she went to give him his first pill, she shook it out into her hand. She knew immediately that she was in trouble. She was able to grab the telephone as she slipped to the floor and punched operator. Before she lost consciousness, she was able to tell the operator her address. (This was before 911.) Fortunately, help arrived soon enough to revive her and she recovered fully in the hospital. When she was referred to me we discussed treatment options, limited mostly to avoidance. I was not about to test her even in a hospital setting, and so she began taking her allergy problem even more seriously than she had in the past.

Dr. Lawrence

As Chief of Allergy and Immunology at St. Agnes Hospital, I went to meetings for the national hospital accreditation committee. At one meeting a very elderly physician was conducting the proceedings. He asked us all to introduce ourselves and then he would ask questions about our service, how it was run, etc. When he got to me, I gave him my name and title, with a little tittering from the group. He then asked me how long I had been associated with the hospital. The group laughed because most of them knew my association was lifelong. I told him I had been born here. He paused a moment and then asked me the name of my obstetrician. By some miracle

I actually knew the answer and I replied, "Dr. Lawrence." He chuckled and said that he and Dr. Lawrence had been partners many years ago. He did not remember me and did not expect that I would remember him! The crowd of doctors was highly amused.

The HMO

For several years I was on the panel of a large HMO, but not as a "Preferred Provider". I was not happy about this but my complaints fell on deaf ears at the insurance company. Then the phone rang with a call from the director of the HMO who was in need of an allergist to see a pediatric patient. Would I be willing to see the patient? This family had a PPO type policy. Of course I was willing to see the patient, but was unable to keep from once again indicating my annoyance with the company for not including me on the PPO panel. The rest of the story is obvious. I was immediately added to the panel and subsequently saw many PPO insured patients from the company.

Five Hips

Midway through his hospital stay for his first hip replacement, my father-in-law turned 65 years old. From then on, his dining room table was covered with papers relating to the surgery and who got to pay what. Left to his own devices, he finally got it figured out so that Medicare got to pay for his second hip replacement. I remember visiting him at the White Plains Hospital Medical Center where I was Chief of Allergy immediately after his first surgery. In my mind the new hip was probably made out of leather and wood. When I came into his room, I could see all the normal IVs running and the other wires leading to various machines. In addition there was one IV line running up under his sheets in the vicinity of his hip surgery. I was much concerned since infection at the operative site was a serious complication. Indeed, antibiotics were being dripped directly into the site of the operation. Eventually he was sent home with a perfectly good artificial hip, having undergone the first such hip surgery in that hospital.

A couple of years later he had his second hip done. This was titanium and very modern. No post-op problems this time but Grandpa fell one day and broke, of all things, the new hip! This was easily fixed by another replacement. New York State took away his disabled parking spot at the World Trade Center and he had to resume the old commute from New Rochelle by train. Grandpa Cunningham went to his grave having had a total of five hips in his lifetime.

$10.00 Brain Tumor

Everyone has heard horror stories about the antics of HMOs. One of my patients actually showed up in the office on the day I knew she was to have surgery. She had been prepped for surgery early in the morning and, while waiting, lying on the gurney outside the operating room, her doctor arrived to say that her HMO was unwilling to authorize her surgery. So, she left the hospital and came for her allergy treatment instead.

There was one comment however that about summed things up for me as far as HMOs were concerned. I heard a lady happily announce as she was leaving the office after paying her co-pay that, "I can have my allergy shots for $10.00 and I can have my brain tumor removed for $10.00!" Her point was well taken.

Killing Cats

One of my patients, a lovely unmarried lady, lived with three cats. She was extremely sensitive to cat dander. She even knew which cat caused her the most trouble and was able to remove him from her household. However, she continued to have severe symptoms and was treated with the cat antigen available at that time. No one thought it worked very well, but it did seem to help some people a little. Finally, a new cat antigen came on the market for immunotherapy. Rather than just the cat's fur it was made from the pelt proteins and other cat proteins as well. Of course, the cats had to be sacrificed. My patient began treatment with this vaccine which was very potent and had to be administered with extreme caution. She did very well until one day, in the treatment room for her injection she suddenly burst into tears. As soon as she said it was about the new vaccine I knew what was on her mind. Cats would have to be killed in order to produce the new antigen and she felt that therefore she could not be treated with it. I happened to have had the same question myself and so I had learned from the manufacturer that the cats were all obtained after having been euthanized as part of normal animal shelter routine. After discussion, my patient finally agreed to continue treatment. Eventually she was getting treatment at widely spaced intervals and had no symptoms of cat allergy. She even offered my wife and me her house on Cape Cod to use when we wanted to get away but, since my wife is highly allergic to cats and was also receiving therapy, we were unable to take her up on the offer.

Abandoned in the Waiting Room

One of the several offices I had over the years had a waiting room which was not completely visible from the front desk. Waiting room visibility became a necessary design component of the offices after my partner and I had reviewed a legal case for lawyers involving a man who may have succumbed to a reaction to his shots from an office where not all the patients could easily be observed after their treatments. He had been found unconscious in his car at a stoplight in mid-town Manhattan after his treatment and died several weeks later.

However, we did have the office noted above for several years. We left a patient alone in the waiting room when we all left for the day. Thank heavens she was one of our favorite people, a patient long before and after this incident. She said she had finished waiting the prescribed period after her shots, lost in a magazine article and didn't realize she was alone in the office until she went to leave. We did wonder the next day when we found that the door was not double-locked as it ought to have been. We were, of course, very apologetic and she took it in good humor. It became an office procedure to always check the waiting room before we left at the end of office hours.

A Difficult Child

I took care of a girl about 10 years old who was a terror about getting her shots. I'm not even sure how we finally got her skin tests done. Whenever she came to the office and came into the treatment room, she would scream bloody murder, never address me directly, squirming about so that I had to hold onto her as firmly as I dared to complete the treatment. I was never happy about having her in my waiting room. Her mother had been banished from the treatment room since her presence there made the child's behavior worse.

One day I called her in for her shots and she walked calmly into the room, said hello and practically held out her arm for her injection. I chanced a query about how she was feeling and she replied that she had been doing very well. Of course, I immediately asked my nurse what had come over this patient. With a roll of her eyes, she told me that the little girl's teacher was in the waiting room! Thus the sudden change in behavior. When she arrived the next week for her shots, she behaved perfectly even though her teacher was not present. I said to her, "I've got you now, don't I?" She agreed that I did and she never gave anyone in the office the least trouble again.

The Shirt-tail

In my Manhattan office I saw quite a few people who were gay. Several of the men even "came out" to me over the years or shared with me stories of their struggles with their sexuality. Careful listening was all that was usually required of me, but, in later years of course, our dialogues always ended with my admonition to "be careful". Richard was such a young man, very attractive and very well groomed. He was always cheerful and pleasant. One day he arrived in the office looking very down. I asked what was the matter since this was so unlike him. He told me that when he left home to come to the office he felt very good about the way he looked and this seemed to be confirmed by the glances of passersby on his way up Park Avenue. But, when he arrived in the vestibule of my building and looked down he saw that his zipper was open and his shirttail was sticking out through his fly! He was mortified and very unhappy when he came into the office. The way he told the story coupled with his unusual demeanor struck me as exceedingly funny and I couldn't help but laugh. I assured him that I was not laughing at him but only at the situation and he was soon laughing along with me. I suppose that to this day he never steps into public view without checking to see that a similar problem does not arise.

Black and Blue

One of my favorite patients was a beautiful southern lady (from Magnolia, Arkansas) who was married to the CEO of a large national company. She was a long-time patient and was very active in hospital affairs as well. In that capacity she also knew my wife who was similarly involved. Thankfully, my patient had a lovely disposition and sense of humor. She received her allergy shots one Thursday afternoon. I next encountered her at the Hospital Ball at The Westchester Country Club on Saturday night. She was wearing a less than flattering gown with open sleeves draped from shoulder to elbow. As we passed each other in the reception room, she flipped up her sleeve to reveal to me a rather large black and blue area, obviously due to her allergy shot. And she said, "I was not planning on wearing this dress tonight!" As she continued on her way, I never even thought to be upset because I knew we would laugh about it at her next office visit. It would also give me a chance to advise her, as I did all my female patients who were going to be someplace where their arms would show, not to come for their treatments until after the affair.

Mrs. B.

When I had been in practice a few weeks, I was asked by a local physician if I would be willing to see an elderly lady who lived during the summer in her house in Scarsdale, N.Y. My job would be to make a house call once a week to take her blood pressure. I was to keep a record but I was never to tell her what the reading was unless she asked and then I was to give her a specific number. I agreed to all this because, in reality, her blood pressure was fine and varied in the normal range. It was the variation which caused her to worry, so I wasn't to mention it.

The day of my first visit arrived and I went to the address I had been given. No one had told me that Mrs. B. was perhaps the wealthiest person in town and that her husband had managed one of the country's largest tobacco fortunes and that he himself had endowed a medical school. She lived on 34 acres in the middle of Scarsdale in a mansion with 21 in help, including four full time grounds keepers. Several of them lived on the estate. Mrs. B. lived by herself in the mansion.

Thus, I was slightly in awe when I pulled into the circular driveway in my little red VW. Trying not to look overly impressed and clutching my little (brown) bag, I rang the bell. A nurse in uniform greeted me and introduced me to Mrs. B. in the grand foyer featuring an elegant circular staircase and art scenes painted on the walls. I was told we would be having our visit in the master bedroom. I was making my way to the stairs when, sensing that I was alone, I turned to see Mrs. B. and her companion standing in front of what I assumed was a closet door. Well, of course, this was the elevator complete with a lovely Louis XIV chair and quite large enough to hold us all.

Upstairs we adjourned to the bedroom which contained the largest four-poster bed I had ever seen. It actually had steps up into it! Over in one corner was a regulation-sized double bed where my new patient actually slept.

We went into an anteroom where I took my patient's blood pressure and happily announced the results. At that visit, we two hit it off. She explained to me that her reaction to Medicare was that she was well enough off not to need it. And she paid her medical bills on time.`

I continued to see this lovely lady for 2 years. She invited my wife and me to accompany her granddaughter on a tour of the house and estate. There was Napoleonic silver service in the dining room and a butler who stood at her side to offer her dishes during her meals. It was a terrific demonstration of "how the other half lives". Mrs. B. finally returned to New York City under the care of Dr. Coffin, a well known internist there. After Mrs. B. died, her estate was sold and divided into building lots for expensive houses. The mansion, however, is still in use as a private home. Driving past there now reminds me of a happy time in the early years of my practice.

The Golfer

I began seeing Mrs. B. right after I opened my practice, at which time I saw medical and allergy patients. Allergy referrals were sparse since the internists, many of whom I frequently covered for, were reluctant to send me allergy patients for fear that they would become my medical patients as well. Eventually I began doing allergy exclusively and business picked up.

One of my more notable patients, to me at least, was a lady who came in early on with a rash on the upper surface of her right index and middle fingers. She showed the rash to me at my desk and the two of us sat there looking at it. I thought, what had I been doing my last year in training, not to be able to recognize this problem. However, it clearly was a contact dermatitis. I do not play golf, but had seen people inserting their tees on the golf course. Inspiration hit suddenly. Yes, the patient's skin did come in contact with the golf course grass when she placed her tees. I advised her to be sure that her skin was not in contact with the turf in future, gave her a little cortisone to rub into the rash and she departed having found the cause of her problem. I was quite happy with myself over this.

Bee Sting Stories

About midway through my career, it became apparent that the immunotherapy for insect stings was not very effective. It did work in some cases however. Fortunately, about that time, really good antigens became available and treatment for possible life-threatening reactions to stings became highly effective.

On the Beach

A young teenage boy had been cavorting on the beach with his friends in front of his summer beach house. The group thought he had decided to take a nap on the sand. When his mother called for him from the house and he did not respond, someone noted that he could not be roused. When he finally regained consciousness in the hospital, he remembered having been stung, and indeed, a sting site was found on his body. One wonders what the outcome would have been had not his condition been noticed and treated correctly and rapidly.

On the Bus

All of my bee-sting patients are instructed to carry adrenalin for self administration in case of a sting in order to gain time enough to get to an appropriate medical setting for treatment. A young man who was in maintenance sting immunotherapy was traveling through Spain with other students during the summertime. A young woman in the back of the bus was stung and immediately began to show signs of a generalized reaction. My patient was there to give her a shot of adrenaline enabling her to get more extensive help and possibly saving her life.

In the Pool

Another patient, the owner of a well-known plastic utensil company was vacationing in Puerto Rico with his wife. She was a nurse. He was in the resort pool when his wife noticed that he had suddenly disappeared under the water. She was able to keep him from drowning when he went rapidly into shock after being stung. Eventually, like most of the others described here, he became a faithful patient with excellent protection.

In the Woods

An older man had been splitting logs in the woods when he was stung. He immediately drove himself home. Luckily, his wife was sitting out on the porch in view of the driveway for, when he exited the car, he collapsed on the gravel. By then 911 was working and he recovered without incident after treatment.

In the Greenhouse

The wife of a board member of one of my hospitals in NYC was showing her minister around her greenhouse in North Carolina one morning. She was stung during the greenhouse tour, collapsed and died immediately so sudden and severe was her reaction. I do not know whether she had had prior reactions to stings.

On the lawn

I began my practice on July 1st. In August, I happened by chance to be working alone in the office on a Saturday afternoon. When the telephone rang, I answered it, forgetting that I was connected to the answering service. A patient of mine reported that he had been stung while mowing his lawn, that he had taken a shower, and was beginning to feel "funny". I got his address, which was nearby and drove to his home where I found him alone, lying on the sofa covered with hives. I administered adrenalin immediately, which took effect quickly. He went to the hospital then to finish recovering. We talked occasionally about the coincidences involved in his story.

While Out Running

In my practice there never was a bee sting reaction more severe than the one for which the patient had been treated originally. Except for one man. I was at a summertime party when I got a call that the patient had been admitted to the hospital. He had not finished his initial treatment regimen and had been somewhat irregular about getting his shots. What did him in however, was running on a very hot summer day and getting stung. He knew he was in trouble immediately, and so, being close by, simply continued running to the hospital emergency room. He recovered, somewhat chastened, and then was a bit more careful about his treatments.

In the Garden

I got a call while in the New York City office about an older man who had been stung, suffered a reaction and was hospitalized. His doctor asked if I would stop in to see him to make sure that his treatment was going correctly. Forgetting about the tie I was wearing (my college tie covered with yellow jackets, the school mascot), I soon found myself talking with the patient and examining his medications. During this procedure I was leaning over the patient a bit when he asked, smiling, whether I wore that particular tie whenever I saw a bee-sting patient. We both had a good laugh over that and the patient by now was almost fully recovered.

Employees

The Transformation

One of the blessings of my practice was the high quality of my helpers and their loyalty. One time, however, I needed to hire a new secretary for the White Plains office. A very pretty but not especially neat-looking young lady came for an interview and I hired her. It soon became apparent that the job was not going to work out for her. This was mainly because of sloppy habits involving her person, dress and the office duties. She was bright enough to do the work, but entirely unmotivated. So, I fired her on a Friday afternoon. When I arrived in the office on Monday, there she was. I assumed that she had misunderstood her position and so I fired her again. Again, she showed up for work in the morning. I didn't know what else to do, so I called her mother. She agreed with everything I had done and said she would enlighten her daughter. That did work. She didn't show up again for work.

About a year later there came a knock on the back door to the office, which I opened. There stood a lovely young woman, beautifully dressed. I stared at her and when she said that I probably didn't recognize her, I suddenly did! Here was the young woman I had fired several times. She was in school now, doing very well and from our talk, seemed to have life well in hand. So, I called her mother. She told me that the best thing that had ever happened to her daughter was the "difficult" experience she had had in my office. Because of it, she decided to turn her life around (with a lot of help from Mom, I bet), and was now on her way to success. If I needed a secretary then, I would have rehired her in a flash. She did not however want her old job back!

Pat

For many years in the New York City office, Pat was the office manager. She was a beautiful black woman, the mother of four fine, grown children and a devout Christian. All of the patients loved her. Here are a couple of my fond memories of Pat.

Pat was always on the telephone. She had to be when the HMOs came in. Otherwise few of the patients' bills would have ever been paid. And, of course, there were HMO approvals and numerous other insurance related problems to be solved. There was a seldom-used loud speaker system in the office. One day while I was in my office in the back, I heard music spilling from the speakers. When I went to investigate, I found Pat filing charts with the telephone receiver off of its cradle. Pat, it turned out, spent so much time on "hold" with the insurance companies, which always played music while Pat waited, that she decided to listen to the music while getting her office work done. She was sure to know when someone came on the line. An efficient use of Pat's time.

I knew that Pat spent most of her weekends at church services. One Monday morning when I came into the office, Pat greeted me in a hoarse voice that could hardly be heard. A little while later, I noticed that she was moving very slowly around the office and even had a slight limp. I knew immediately what had happened. So I called Pat into my office and explained that I applauded her religiosity but that perhaps it would be best if she sat quietly in church on Sundays. Saturdays were fine, but she ought to leave Sunday to recover for work the next day. She immediately burst out laughing as did I while she explained that indeed she had been a bit carried away the day before at church, just as I suspected.

Pat could perfectly well say "ask" because I asked her to, but she never did, preferring "axed" instead.

Pat's daughter and daughter-in-law worked in the office for periods of time and her sons were recruited to do any of the hard stuff around the place such as hanging blinds and moving furniture. Her sons preferred to work in the back of the office since Pat could see just what they were doing up front and would always have something to say about how the work was being done! Believe me, no one ever stepped out of line while Pat was around and most of us did her bidding without really realizing it. When the time came, the man who bought my practice hired Pat to work for him and she subsequently went off to nursing training. To this day, I have no idea how old Pat is for she had such a pretty face and beautiful skin which never changed over the years.

Pat usually wore a long dashiki to work, with boots and a cap. And, she never used an umbrella, declaring that if it was God's will that she get wet with

His rain that would be a good thing. I never saw Pat out of sorts and she was unfailingly kind to the patients. She was and is one of my favorite people.

A Male Employee

Once in awhile a man would call to see if I had a position open. On the rare occasions that I did, I had to tell them that I was unable to hire a male because he and I would be alone in the office from time to time with only a female patient present. Since I never saw a female without a chaperone, I thought it best to keep a female employee nearby. The men inquiring always agreed with me. However, that would not have been the case in the NY office since the female secretary would always be there during office hours. So I did hire a well qualified man to help with the nursing chores. Within a short period of time he had run up a large telephone bill calling 900 numbers, usually at night after we had all gone home, all but filled a separate refrigerator with blood samples which needed testing but were never sent to the lab, and wrote checks for himself on our account, which the bank happily cashed for him, to the tune of $6000.00! (The bank refused to give our money back despite proof of what had happened, so we took our accounts, business and personal, elsewhere.) From then on we didn't even entertain the idea of a male staff member, unfairly, I suppose.

The Cigarette

Needless to say, there was a strict no smoking policy in the office. My nurse/secretary was a chain smoker. She did smoke in the office when hours were not going on, but I never saw her smoke or go out to smoke during office hours. One day I discovered the reason. After she would take all of the trays out of the refrigerator in preparation for office hours, she would place her cigarette in an ash tray in the refrigerator! I have no idea how long she got away with this, but she was asked not do it anymore right then. Several years later, she quit smoking cold turkey. The reason; her 3 year old daughter was suspected of having a serious disease and her mother thought she had better be around to care of her in the future. Thankfully, the diagnosis on the child did not pan out, but my aide never did take up smoking again.

The Pink Curler

Another time, I advertised for a receptionist. One lady arrived for her interview. She was a mature, white haired lady whose sole noticeable feature was an enormous pink curler set in the middle of the top of her head. It was all I could do to keep from staring and even harder to ask why she had shown up for a job interview in this condition. I didn't hire her.

Lois

I hired a woman to be the office secretary and to help in the lab. I have no idea how things would have turned out because in her first and only month's work for me she was absent without prior notice five times. One Thursday morning when I arrived in the office she was not there again but her shoes were under the desk! I found my wife at a hospital board meeting and asked her to come to work for afternoon office hours. Then I thought, Lois had said something to me about wanting to work. She, her three boys and her husband had been patients of mine for several years by then. So, I got her chart out and called her at home. When I asked if she would like to come to work for me that afternoon, she replied, "I'm standing here with my coat over my arm!"

Indeed, she did show up for work that afternoon and started being trained by me and Peggy. When I retired 10 years later, the doctor who bought my practice hired her. Recently, Lois also retired after she had worked in the office for 17 years! I literally do not remember that she missed a single day of work that wasn't a holiday or vacation day. Lois had been a school teacher, a fact that was clear to me when I read the sign she had posted, in perfect printing, at her window. "Hi! I'm Lois, what's your name?" All those years later, the same sign was still there.

Lois is a lovely woman, very bright and full of ideas and a fashion plate in the bargain. I am happy to say that we are still the best of friends—she and her husband come to see us when they are in Baltimore and we go to them for Seder. Truly one of the nicest relationships to come out of my practice.

Betty

Betty is a beautiful woman who worked in the office for many years. She was not able to do lab work, because, as she said, she never learned how. Everyone loved her. Her son eventually went to medical school and used the microscope I used in medical school. When I first arrived on the scene, the office was in my eventual partner's house. My first day on the job, just out of training, I was alone, the doctor having gone on vacation. Betty, always there, was also missing, so the secretary from New York was manning the desk. A mother and her son, the patient, arrived and settled down in the living room. They didn't see anyone they recognized, and soon, I stuck my head out of the office (sun room) to call a patient in. At that point, the patient was heard to say to his mother, "Are we in the right office?" They were but there was no one around whom they had ever seen before. Another time, Dr. Brown was away again, having left me in charge. I saw his new and old patients for several weeks. One patient asked me, in all seriousness, "Is there a Doctor Brown?" I thought this very funny, but assured her that he would shortly be back and she would have a laying-on of the eyes pretty soon.

Queen

I had a secretary in the New York office, Queen, who was a statuesque light-skinned black woman. She was an excellent employee, but I really never did get over her name. One day I was talking by phone with my granddaughter who was living in Lagos, Nigeria at the time and who attended The American School there. I asked if she had made any new friends. She said that, indeed, she had—there was Pierre, he was from Paris, and Nicole, she was from London and there was Queen, she was black, she was from Detroit. What a laugh we all had over that!

The Holidays

When I returned from a vacation I noticed a new person at the front desk. Rather than ask how my time off had gone, my partner frantically waved me into his room as I went toward my office. He had hired the new lady, who was an observant Jew, only to find that, in addition to the usual holidays, she required time off for all of the Jewish holidays as well. They numbered somewhere in the twenties. Of course, it would not have been possible to run the office correctly with her absent so much of the time. My partner should have been conversant with this sort of problem but, since he did not practice his religion to this degree, it did not occur to him. He was concerned about firing her, possibly because of religious concerns. I told him I would take care of it. I asked the new employee to come back to my office and there I explained to her that my partner and I had a contract which clearly stated that neither one of us could hire or fire anyone without the other's consent. This was true. Since I didn't consent to her being hired, she was free to go. She left without any problem. My partner tried to get me to tell him what I had done, but he was never able to worm it out of me, a little joke of my own there, I suppose.

Dr. C.

Soon after my partner retired it became obvious that I would need help running my practice. I called the executive secretary of my training institute to see if she had any ideas about who might come to work for me. She immediately named Dr. C, a young resident just finishing up his training. We hit it off immediately; he was enthusiastic, I knew he was very well trained and he was highly recommended. So he came to work for me and took a great load off my mind and the burden of trying to do everything myself. He had one problem however. He was tall, dark and very handsome! But, since it didn't bother me a bit when the young single business women would politely ask if they could see Dr. C. for their treatments instead of me, he became a significant asset to the practice. The internationally known doctor who bought my practice hired him and continues to employ him these many years later.

Celebrities

There was an ENT physician in Manhattan just up Park Avenue from my office who sent a great number of referrals to us over the years. They were almost all well known people and we used to kid around saying that if we had to have a celebrity in the office in 10 minutes, all we had to do was go up and get the first person we saw out of this doctor's waiting room and bring him/her to our office. Once, Paul Newman called, which created a stir among the ladies in my office. And once, Elizabeth Taylor actually made an appearance. Interest ran high as her appointment approached. When she arrived, she turned out to be several inches taller than expected, several years older, clearly not the actress we had been expecting. Eventually the list of real celebrities got rather long. Most were ordinary nice people and we treated them just as if they were perfectly ordinary. However, several left us holding the bag with unpaid bills and some were unable to cope with just being ordinary. Some were difficult patients, demanding and unwilling to cooperate with our care. Some were highly entertaining. Several stand out. One singer, who now is quite famous, eventually didn't pay the $300.00 she owed to me. To this day, I am tempted to try to catch up with her (her performance schedule is well known) and remind her about that. Another, still active actress arrived looking positively unattractive, with no makeup and her hair uncombed. Even now, when I see her on TV I marvel at the wonders of cosmetics and hair styling done with taste. My last contact with her occurred when she called me on a Saturday morning, via her office patch from half-way across the globe where she was filming. She had been in an "explosion" scene and it had affected her nose and what should she do about that for immediate relief. The conversation developed into a minor set-to and that was that.

A Star of Stage and Screen

There are certain celebrities who are instantly recognizable by their looks, style of dress, voice, etc. One celebrity, more recognizable than most, came into the office as a patient. She turned out to be a good patient and fun to have around. Her first request however was that we should call her by her married name. We all thought that this was a fascinating idea since anyone who had ever gone to the movies, seen a musical or watched TV was sure to know who she was by her voice alone. Not to mention her hairdo. After her first treatment, following which she needed to wait for 20 minutes as all patients did before leaving the office, she asked if she could use an unoccupied examining room. We agreed. Shortly thereafter, passing the room with its door open, I saw her peering intently at a tiny scrap of paper held tightly between her thumb and forefinger while she made dainty, small steps, all the time standing nearly in place. I hadn't a clue until it dawned on me that she was practicing a dance step. Since this became a routine of hers, we were delighted to have her use a room for this purpose and wondered if we would ever see any of this performed in another venue.

Another time, one of the few early mornings when I arrived later than usual at the office (but not late), there she stood opposite the elevator door on my office floor encouraging me in her distinctive voice to hurry up so as not to be late or to have her be late for her next appointment. I have often chuckled about what the other riders on the elevator with me that morning were thinking as the car continued on its upward journey. Probably just that it was just another interesting start to a day in New York City.

The Diva

A well-known African-American opera star was a patient of mine. At one of her visits, she brought along her husband who was white. One afternoon she received her treatments without ill effect and left the office. That evening, at home, I received a call from her distraught-sounding husband. Had I seen the woman? Yes, I had, but I had not heard from her since she left the office. Eventually, by what means I do not know, her husband found her in England. She had left the office, and without telling anyone, hopped a flight to the UK. It was the last time I ever saw her in person, but not the last time I saw her perform. I later heard that the marriage had failed. I was not surprised!

Augusta

Although she was not strictly a "celebrity", she was one in my book. One of the finest, most aristocratic women that I have known, she was my partner's mother. Twice widowed, Augusta lived near 58th Street on Sixth Avenue in Manhattan. Among other things, she was a gifted painter of Chinese scenes, a world traveler and an avid golfer. Two of her watercolors hung in my home. In her 80's, she would lug her golf clubs by herself on the subway to the public course at the end of the line in Tremont, the Bronx, play a round of golf and return home by the same route. Both coming and going involved long fights of subway stairs.

There came a time when China opened up to foreign travelers. One day Augusta arrived in the office and announced that she wanted to talk to Bill. Her son rolled his eyes at that, but Augusta and I adjourned to an examining room to chat. She immediately announced that she had "ennui". Having no idea what she meant, I inquired as to the cause of this feeling which was so out of character for her. She told me that, at the age of 87, she had told her internist that she was going to China. He immediately forbade her to do so. She was very down and even depressed over this. All I could think to say was that she had made a very serious mistake. At that she perked up, wondering what I meant. I explained that the mistake was telling her physician about her plans. She seemed to take that under consideration and left shortly after getting her usual follow-up on my children.

Several months later a similar scenario took place, only this time Augusta was in high spirits. I remember clearly how she said to me, "Bill, I'm going to China!" I knew immediately that her physician had not been informed and that my partner had given his blessing. So, off she went. About a month later, after completing the whole tour and having caught one of the respiratory illnesses that many travelers brought home from China with them, Augusta was taken from her return flight directly to Lenox Hill Hospital to recover, I think, from pneumonia. I remember arriving in her room for a visit where it was very dark and various machines and IVs were running. She looked at me with the happiest smile, as sick as she was, and said, "Well, I've been to China." I could not have been happier for her. Her recovery was speedy and she was able shortly to return to her apartment.

Not long after this, as I was going into my building in the morning I saw this little figure wearing a bonnet and carrying a straw bag striding toward me. I knew it was Augusta. I couldn't help telling her that she looked a little like a refugee coming along in that outfit and we had a good laugh. She was on her way to her painting lesson.

S&S

I took care of a very famous playwright and a theater critic almost as well known. They were not good friends. One afternoon, my secretary came to tell me that they were both in the waiting room at the same time. While I thought it was hilarious, I had her call the first one to arrive out of the waiting area. By the time we were finished his nemesis was safely ensconced in another treatment room. I did not press the waiting for 20 minutes after injections rule, so that by the time I was done with the second patient, the critic, the playwright was gone. Thus was avoided a clash of artists. I noted that they never were seen together again, arranging their schedules so as to get their treatments on separate days, I suppose. (One note: Neither of these men ever produced a ticket to anything for the staff, not even a twofer even though I saw them weekly for several years. Another patient, a Broadway producer never arrived without tickets of some sort. Sometimes he brought so many we left them on the counter for other patients to use!)

The Cardinal

My partner was Jewish and my New York office manager at the time was Jewish. But, I was on vacation when a Cardinal of the Church came to the office. He was dressed as an ordinary Catholic clergyman. There ensued a discussion about what to call the Cardinal when his turn to be seen came. My partner and my nurse, a good Catholic, had no idea but, my office manager said, finally, she guessed that "Your Eminence" would be correct. How she knew this I never did find out, but when I heard the story I said that simply calling him Father would have been sufficient. Well, no one believed that, so, at his next visit, I asked His Eminence outright about how to address him, and the problem that had caused. He said that he would have been pleased to have been called Father, since that, after all was what he was, but that "Your Eminence" was correct as well. We all had a good laugh over this and it would come up from time to time when a patient insisted on being called by his or her title and no one could remember what it was! Unlike many other offices, to this day I address patients by their titles, not by their first names

The Orchestra Conductor

One of my favorite patients was a well known orchestra conductor in New York City. A sunny personality with an ability to accept criticism endeared her to me. On the rare occasions when negative comments were printed about a performance of her orchestra, I usually commented to her on something that had been said in the review. She would then explain the comment to me and we would end up laughing about it. Over the years, in different places, I have met singers and other conductors, some of whom know her personally and all of whom have heard about her.

The Monsieur

A man from Laos, small in stature but large on the world scene was "The Monsieur". He came to me with very bad, lifelong asthma. Newer drugs were becoming available and he was a totally compliant patient who did extremely well on a carefully crafted medical regimen. Monsieur was in charge of United Nations troops in much of the world. He had two stunningly beautiful daughters with astronomically high IQs. I knew he continued to do well after I retired when he and his wife came to visit us in our new home in Florida. Monsieur travelled the world and I have many gifts which he would bring to the office for me. Reminders of a truly lovely man.

National Disasters

The World Trade Center I

Just about everyone remembers where they were and what they were doing when great disasters occur. Everyone old enough can probably remember the Kennedy assassination and their personal circumstances at the time. One chilly day in February, 1992, I was driving home from the New York City office at my usual time in the early afternoon. It was snowing lightly and the weather was quite unpleasant. I began to notice a great number of fire engines and emergency rescue trucks speeding south on the opposite side of the Major Deegan Expressway toward the City. My first thought was that they were on their way to a show of some sort. However, when I turned onto the Bronx River Parkway, which is normally used by passenger vehicles only, ambulances and other equipment were speeding south on that roadway, too. I began to think that this might represent a disaster response and mentioned this to my wife when I got home. Soon thereafter of course we learned of the first bombing of the World Trade Center. I remember hearing and seeing in the newspaper and on television clips of the massive numbers of vehicles all around the site and thinking that I had seen a great many of them speeding by me.

Oklahoma City

At my clinic in the South Bronx there was a large television set in the waiting room. I was quite used to hearing the drone of the set. The patients waiting were almost always very quiet, watching TV or engrossed in their own thoughts. On May 19, 1995 in the late morning, I heard a collective gasp coming from the waiting area. Thinking someone was not well, I went to check. The image on the TV screen completely arrested my progress into the area and I stood with the others to try to discover what had happened and where. Another time I will always remember where I was and what I was doing.

In-air Emergencies

The Broken Leg

The one and only time I ever flew for free was on a flight to Denver, CO, courtesy of a drug company which was hosting a medical meeting to introduce new products. I was seated next to a woman who steadfastly ignored me. Having an aisle seat made it easy for me to get about without having to engage her. Eventually, I made my way to the rear bathroom. While inside, I thought I heard the PA system come on, but all I could make out was "or nurse". When I came out of the bathroom, I had a view of the entire airplane. No one was moving about or loitering anywhere. I asked the nearest attendant about what I had heard although I was beginning to suspect what it was. Indeed, they were looking for a doctor or nurse and I was just the ticket.

The cabin crew led me to a woman seated with her leg precariously elevated and wrapped in ice. The flight crew had done a creditable job caring for the lady. Her history soon made it clear that she was in big trouble. She had fallen while boarding the plane and by now her leg was hugely swollen and purple. She said she was flying on to Hawaii. This, I knew, was not about to happen this day. I asked the attendants to tell the pilot to be sure there was a wheel-chair to meet the woman in Denver and that she would have to be taken to a hospital. The pilot was not happy about all of this, but he had no choice.

I returned to my seat. My seatmate burst into conversation about who I was and what I had done, which amused me greatly. What did not amuse me was the offer by the attendant to give me a free drink by way of a thank you. There I was on a flight where my drinks were free anyway being offered a free drink! Just my luck, I guess.

The Coronary

So, there we were, traveling with Dr. H., an internist and his wife, flying high over the Atlantic Ocean in the middle of the night on our way to Frankfurt, Germany. My friend, a medical school classmate who had been my best man and his wife were fast asleep. I have never slept a wink on an airplane so I easily heard the request for a doctor. I asked my friend to come with me to see about an older lady who was ill in the next compartment of the 747. It was clear that she was having serious trouble but examining her in the plane was a challenge. We administered oxygen and then communicated to the pilot that we had better land as soon as possible. I will never forget the conversation with him on the upper deck. He was not happy saying that we had probably flown beyond a landing at Shannon, Ireland. But, he would do his best to comply with our wishes. In a short while, we did land at Shannon and an Irish physician in his tweed coat, with two assistants, boarded the plane and removed the patient and her husband who had been on their way to India. My wife and I had bulkhead seats and soon after we began to settle down and were airborne again, an attendant arrived and sat on the fold-down seat in front of us. I asked if anyone had complained about the unscheduled landing and, to my surprise, she said that a man in First Class was irate. I offered to settle his hash for her, but she laughingly declined. Then she revealed that many older people were always on this flight terminating in New Delhi, often already ill and going home to India to die. She was very happy that we had insisted on landing since during a similar incident the week before a doctor and the pilot agreed to fly on to Frankfurt. The patient, a man who was having a coronary, died on the approach to the airport. It was a sad story but increased my confidence that what Dr. H and I had done was the right thing. On the way home, we got to wondering how our patient had done, but we were not able to figure out a way to find out.

In the Clinic

The Hallucination

I have been in a lot of places, but, so far as I know, I have only been in one person's hallucination.

From my office desk in my clinic in the south Bronx, I could see a lady waiting patiently to come in. I called her into the office and asked her where she had been because it had been quite some time since she had last visited the clinic. She replied that she had been in the mental hospital for several months. We talked about that for a while and then she told me that I had been in her hallucination. She told me a little about that, much of which I didn't understand. We both laughed however when I told her that this was a new experience for me and that I would take being in her hallucination as a compliment. I had the idea that she was much improved mentally and I hoped that she would stay that way.

Plain and Fancy Ladies

In one of my clinics I regularly saw a lady who always dressed in the plainest clothes imaginable. One day I needed to examine her chest and asked her to remove the top of her outfit. I managed to avoid rolling my eyes, unlike my nurse-chaperone, when I discovered that my patient had on very frilly, not to say sexy, undergarments. Later, a similar event occurred except that this time I was dealing with a very stylish, rather sexy woman. To my surprise, this lady was wearing cotton underwear which did nothing to enhance her allure. Afterward, my nurse and I discussed what the reasons between the inner and outer appearances of these two women might be. In future, my nurse would signal to me that there was likely a similar surprise waiting for me with other patients.

I Know I'm Dying . . .

For several years, I also saw a very pleasant middle-aged lady whom I knew to have a very serious disease outside of my specialty. I felt so upset for her when, one day, she said, "I know I'm dying, it's just that it's taking so long." It was a very difficult remark to respond appropriately to.

In White Face

One of my favorite clinic patients was Mrs. D. She dressed entirely in black, I know not why, and used stark white, stage-type makeup on her face. She was a tiny, older lady but quite pleasant. Only in New York, I suppose.

And then there was the lady who showed up in my clinic one day wearing one blue and one brown shoe. How she and I laughed about that. It often came up in our visits, too, and remained a source of good humor.

We are speaking French!

One day my Chief of Medicine at Our Lady of Mercy Hospital called to ask if I would be willing to fill in for a colleague who ran the allergy clinic in the Morrissania area of the Bronx who had become ill and would not be able to work for a while. It was a very poorly paid position. I said that I would be happy to substitute for a few weeks. In the end, I stayed for 15 years at a much better pay rate.

It soon became apparent to me that my lack of knowledge of Spanish was going to be a drawback despite having translators readily available. So I began taking Spanish lessons at night school in White Plains at the high school. About two months into that, I noted during one clinic session that most of the staff was hanging around my office. With my aide/translator at my side I began seeing a young woman and her elderly mother who was the patient. I began the history asking questions of the daughter and waiting for her to translate her mother's answers. It was slow going. I turned to my aide and said, "It's a good I am taking Spanish lessons." Whereupon, the young daughter drew herself up and, quite offended, announced, "We are speaking French!"

Of course, all the people standing nearby burst out laughing, as did I. Even my patient's daughter smiled. The staff knew exactly what was going to happen when I saw these two ladies. It turned out that they were speaking

Creole. I couldn't help but note that these people must be the last two French-speaking people in the neighborhood.

(Eventually, I learned enough Spanish to eliminate the need for a translator except for those times when the patient or I clearly did not understand what the other was trying to say.)

The Subway

In the course of my travels around the Bronx and Manhattan, my rudimentary knowledge of Spanish did come in handy. When approached with "Cambio, cambio?" I rapidly learned to say, "No tengo!" Even that much of the language would send the solicitors on to other likely looking contributors.

Once I was approached while riding the subway by the son of a clinic patient of mine. To his question, "Doc, what are you doing here?" I replied, "Everybody got to be someplace." (From an old joke about the lady who found a little old man in her bedroom closet.)

Spanish

It never fails to amuse me that my Spanish-speaking patients always said "Nueva York" and "New Hersey". That combination could have at least produced "New York". Often these people would laugh at this, too, but kept right on with their usual pronunciation. Also, the Dominican Republic, I soon learned, was the "DR".

When I went to Spain, my clinic personnel all laughed and said that no one there would be able to understand my New York City Spanish. Well, I tried it out on the taxi driver from the airport who either understood my version of Spanish or spoke English. I also discovered that, during siesta, the high school kids were often left in charge of things. They had no trouble at all with my Spanish. However, I did have a little problem in an exclusive linen shop in Madrid when my wife tried to buy a bib for a new nephew. No one there knew any English, but I did manage to make myself well enough understood to buy what we wanted.

Shingles

The day before we left on our trip to Spain, my wife noticed a slight rash on my back. I had had some achiness there following a long session in the garden getting things settled before our trip. By the time we got to Spain it was clear that I had Shingles. At one point, as I was coming out of the shower my wife took one look and called our friend Dr. H. with whom we were again travelling to come ASAP to have a look. He announced that that was the worst case of Herpes Zoster he had ever seen! Since I did all the driving, I needed to be alert and so I decided to try to get some pain medicine that wouldn't knock me out. To everyone's surprise, in Spanish, I eventually talked the hotel doctor into writing me a prescription. He sent us to real pharmacy, after hours, where we found two ladies waiting to escort me into the shop. The prescription had already been filled and so then I had a tour of the lovely little place, all dark wood, multiple levels of drawers and extremely clean preparation areas. All this time I was conversing, sort of, in Spanish. Eventually the medicine did help a bit, but I toured Spain holding my shirt away from my chest whenever I wasn't driving.

Limpio

I frequently wore a white shirt to the office and clinic. The Spanish ladies would have a look at the way I was dressed and would comment, "Muy limpio!" referring to the fact that I was dressed in suit and tie and looked clean and neat. Milagros was one of the great Spanish ladies who helped me with my language skills and was a fan of the way I dressed. She certainly couldn't afford the gifts she gave me, and I suspect that her children and grandchildren, who were very attentive to her, got talked into buying small things for me.

One day, on my way to the clinic I was driving on the Grand Concourse in the Bronx. At one of the huge intersections, I came to a red light. There was a green van in front of me. The light changed but the van didn't move. Why I didn't honk at it I will never know. However, I didn't and suddenly the van swerved quickly to the left across the intersection and was T-boned by a car coming in the opposite direction. The van tipped over and the driver clambered out of his window. I pulled to the side, got out and carefully locked my car to go and see what the condition of the other driver was. In this short period of time, it seemed like hundreds of people were in, on or approaching the wrecked car. It occurred to me later that I was probably the only person in suit and tie for blocks around. The crowd parted as a result of my being "limpio" I suppose and I looked into the car. It was plain that the driver was dead, his blood dripping onto the roadway.

I gave a statement to the police and over the next few weeks had to fill out numerous forms for them. I have always been thankful that I didn't toot at the green van since then I would have felt responsible for this fatal accident.

The Shower

I took care of a lovely Spanish lady whose daughter was also a patient. I commented once that my daughter and her three sisters-in-law loved to sit around the kitchen table "doing" their nails. I also commented on the number of showers they took. She laughed and told me that in her house, an apartment with one bathroom, the shower was always running—24/7. She had six daughters all of whom lived at home and took, she thought, an average of three showers per day. With hair washing as well. After that I never complained about how the bathroom was used in my house.

The Retirement Years

Once a Doctor, Always a Doctor

I hadn't been retired in Florida very long before a lovely, talented lady of my acquaintance called to ask if she could come to speak to me about a medical problem. I had already decided that if this sort of thing happened I would be available but I would limit my advice to just talking, not diagnosing or treating. She arrived bearing a lab report and told me that one doctor had said that she had arthritis and another that she had multiple myeloma. There is a world of difference between these two diagnoses, the former not usually fatal and with many treatment options, the latter almost always fatal and with few good treatments. Naturally, she wanted to have arthritis at this point. However, the lab report she produced was absolutely diagnostic of myeloma. (I can't imagine what the first doctor was thinking.) My advice was for her to obtain a third opinion. She did, was treated expertly only to die about three years later from her disease.

One of the biggest problems for me was knowing what was going on medically with individuals in our group of friends, when no one knew that I was privy to the facts. I managed to field some pretty prying and sometimes insightful questions, even including the occasional comment to the effect that I had known all along, hadn't I?

Another friend came to me one day to discuss what he should do about his prostate cancer. We reviewed the options and he finally decided with my blessing to have brachiotherapy somewhere on the west coast. I really didn't understand why he needed to travel so far, but in the end he did well.

Early on I got to know a lovely gentleman from Canada. Though I did not play golf, he and I always ended up chatting at our weekly pre-Elks cocktail party. He developed a cough, diagnosed as bronchitis. The physician told him to go to the hospital if the cough had not improved in thirty-six hours. He brought the x-ray report to the house for me to look at. It was clear that more than bronchitis was going on. I suggested that he go to the hospital right then. Six weeks later he died of asbestosis (mesothelioma) in Canada. I think of him fondly still.

At a party around a friend's pool, an older gentleman, the Colonel, apparently turned away from the bar too quickly and began to fall over backward. By luck I was standing nearby and I simply stretched out my arm to break his fall and lowered his head gently to the concrete lanai floor. I hardly knew what I had done myself and few others noted the maneuver while the Colonel collected himself and was helped to his feet uninjured except for his dignity. The following morning, he and his wife called to tell me how thankful they were that I was able to "save" the man. I'm sure hitting his head would not have had a good result but my action was totally spontaneous and unworthy of any praise.

One man who was a dear friend long before I retired and still is, Dick Grant, was having trouble with his knees. So, he went to the doctor to see about this problem, telling the doctor about only one knee. This, he informed us all one evening was because he was afraid that the doctor would charge him twice. So, Dick treated both knees the same way which seemed to work for each knee because he went on to become a champion barefoot water skier in his middle 70's!

Even now, having been away from Florida for five years, I occasionally get a call from one or another of my "old" friends. I am always happy to discuss their medical problems in general terms, give encouragement and suggestions on how to proceed when I can. I carefully avoid any specifics and happily acknowledge my lack of expertise when that is necessary.

The Popcorn Club

By the time we settled in Florida we had met most of our friends' friends. These people had formed a social group called The Popcorn Club. Originally meant as an evening at the Club for dinner once every two weeks, it soon became obvious that the hostesses were vying with one another to serve the best hors d'oeuvres at increasing expense at the before-dinner cocktail parties. Lots of people ate a lot of these and didn't go for dinner, defeating the purpose of the Club. So a decree from the founders went forth that only popcorn could be served during cocktail hour. Hence, the name of the Club.

Originally quite exclusive with regard to members, we wondered if we would make the grade for membership in the Club. Our best friends finally had. In late August after we had moved to Plant City in July, a friend asked us to come with her and her husband to Popcorn. We thanked her for the invitation and she informed us that it wasn't really an invitation since we had already been voted in. I asked who cast that deciding vote and she replied, "I did." And so began many evenings of fun which gave Peggy and me a way to get to know many other people, an advantage since I do not play golf.

Upon settling into our new house in Delaware, we thought we would give starting a Popcorn Club a try. Five years later it is a huge success. We rotate hosts and everyone brings a heavy hors d'oeuvre. The hosts supply the drinks and there is virtually no cleanup since everyone takes their platters home. There is now a Popcorn golf group, a tennis group, and an occasional cruise. Most of the people involved never would have known each other without The Popcorn Club.

The Podiatrist

When I retired the first time, we moved to Plant City, Florida, named for Henry B. Plant who built the first railroad across the peninsula, and home to The Strawberry Festival, one of the largest festivals in North America. Since we already had friends there and had met many of their friends and were soon into a few activities, we quickly got to know many people. One of them was Marty, a podiatrist who became a very good friend, despite our age difference and who literally kept me on my feet for many years. He had been practicing in town for about 15 years, had a very large following and was very outgoing. One day in his office as he was carving away at my feet, he suddenly asked how it was that I knew so many people in town after such a short time living there. He said that every time he said Dr. Hermance, someone was sure to say, "Oh, you mean Peggy's husband" and if he mentioned Peggy he would hear, "Oh, you mean Dr. Bill's wife". I thought this was very funny given the fact that he actually did know virtually everyone in town. To this day, Peggy and I wonder what some people are doing in their houses, since they do not seem to ever be away from home or have visitors. We are not that way!

Gray's Anatomy

One of the best things about living in Delaware is being able to see our youngest grandchildren frequently. They are as at home with us as they are at their own house around the corner.

I was sitting on the floor in my library while my granddaughter and I were looking up some things for a class project of hers. My old medical school books are assigned to shelves near the floor where the shelves are larger to accommodate the tomes. While we were doing our research, Caroline suddenly said to me, "Oh! You have Gray's Anatomy! That is one of my mother's favorite programs!" How times change and spellings, too. The program is Grey's Anatomy.

Everyone Around Here Is Sick

While my grandson's other grandfather was in the hospital, Grandma had a bad episode with her diabetes, and Grammy, my wife, had just had a knee replaced. I was still on my feet which were in as bad shape as ever, when I noted in my granddaughter Caroline's presence that I had to go see my doctor (podiatrist). I realized my mistake when said granddaughter complained loudly that "everybody around here is sick!" She sounded quite annoyed.

A Medical Demonstration

Caroline's brother Blake, age three, gave us all a demonstration of what was a new medical problem for Grandpa, a coronary requiring bypass surgery. Apparently Blake had heard a lot about this and knew that Grandpa's chest was somehow involved. Most of the family was assembled one day while Grandpa was still hospitalized when Blake announced that he knew what was wrong with Grandpa. With that, he proceeded to lift up his shirt, grab his nipples and, while pulling them up and down none too gently said, "These things aren't working right." Trying not to seem too amused, we assured him that he definitely had the right idea.

Amnesia

When Caroline was about six years old, Grandpa had an episode of global amnesia, similar to one described previously in one of my patients. Fortunately, it cleared rapidly without any residual effects, but Caroline heard a lot about how he had lost his memory for a while. I was still living in Florida and so I wasn't in on much of this. One day about a year later as I was driving Caroline home from school along our usual route, she said from the back seat that this was not the right way home. I assured her that it was, only to have her protest about it again. I said, "You must have amnesia." Then, thinking that that was a pretty big word I asked if she knew what amnesia was. To my astonishment, she replied, "That would be short-term memory loss." This from a first grader. Apparently the reason for this medical knowledge was left over from her Grandpa's memory problem.

Shanghaied

After I had been enjoying retirement for about 7 years, and after we had settled down in Delaware, my daughter-in-law asked me one day if I would have a look at Caroline who had not been feeling well. I examined her as I had done before on occasion and said, "I don't see much here. If you want Dr. K. to see her tomorrow, that would be fine with me." Caroline's mother took Caroline to see Dr. K. the next day. After looking her over, Dr. K. said to Tricia, "I don't see much here." "That's what my father-in-law said," Tricia remarked. "Is your father-in-law a physician?" Dr. K. inquired. Tricia told her I was an allergist and thought nothing more of it.

While we were having pizza the following Sunday evening with the kids at their house, Dr. K. called, presumably about Caroline who, by this time, was fine. A very odd conversation ensued to which I paid little attention but which puzzled my son, given that he could not figure out what Dr. K. was saying. At length, Tricia said that yes, I was right there and could come to the phone. It was Dr. K. and her husband Dr. K. (Mr. K. in the office, Babu to me) who wanted to know if I could come to talk to them about working part time. As a Board Certified allergist, they were interested in having me in their practice. After an excellent offer, I went to work for four hours twice weekly. (This left me with five day weekends.) So I was happy to find a fully functional allergy clinic being run by a classically trained allergist. My colleague has left, my work time increased to 12 hours weekly and I have an office and two dedicated treatment rooms and lots of help when I need it. I even do a little pediatrics when needed (more malpractice expense) but I draw the line at itty bitty babies. I tell everyone that I was shanghaied but really I love being back at work with no business or on-call responsibilities for a change. My patients are just as rewarding to work with as before and I have already begun adding some of my experiences to these Tales. The office is entirely internally computerized and this is no longer the challenge for me that it was at first.

Happy Harry's

I answered my telephone in the office to hear a woman asking to have a prescription renewed. I brought up the fax form on the computer and asked what she needed. I typed in the prescription and then asked her to which drugstore I should send it. She replied, "Happy Harry's." (This is a huge drugstore chain in our area.) So, I asked her which Happy Harry's. She replied, "The one right here." How is it possible not to get a kick out dealing with the public?

Sex?

There is a long list of questions which patients must answer when they come for their school/sports physical exams in my office. One concerns what one's religion is. One of my teenagers who was there with his father ran aground on this question. His father filled in for him. "Soccer", his father said. Another question asks about sexual activity. The young ones check "no", the older teens check "yes" or "no". My favorite answer however, which I see occasionally, is "n/a". I usually take that for a yes answer.

Two Mommies

Almost unheard of in White Plains, NY and rarely seen in Manhattan while I was in practice were racially mixed parents and same-sex couples. Some say that these two things are prevalent here because of the huge Air Force Base in Dover, DE. The C5 Galaxies fly out of here. I'm not sure that is the reason but, I have had to get used to these life styles as well as an enormous number of separated and divorced couples. The mixed race couples often have quite stable families and well cared for children. I do have trouble hearing a child call an obvious woman "Daddy", but I try not to roll my eyes. So far, I have not had two men as parents together. The real problems come when one parent gets after another because of their differing child care styles. It can be dangerous as well—one parent's house is smoke-free for the asthmatic child while in the other people smoke around the child, in their cars and homes, during visitations. Or, one house has a cat which causes symptoms for the child. My policy is to have the parent write letters to the offending parent and, often, to the lawyers and the court. Then I edit them to be sure they are factual and print them on office stationery. That way I can be sure that the pertinent information is accurately communicated.

Ringworm

While in search of the physician's assistant in the office, I found myself in an examining room with a nurse, two parents, a cute little boy and the assistant. Upon leaving, I patted the little boy on the head. On my way back to my office, I felt an arm go around my shoulder and the quiet voice of the nurse in my ear. "You might want to wash your hands," she said, "He has ringworm of the scalp." I veered off to the nearest bathroom to wash up, thinking that my propensity to be sociable did sometimes have a downside.

The Old Guy

After I had begun my part time work I agreed to see some pediatric patients. The busy office had just lost one pediatrician and things were getting too busy for the other doctors. My malpractice insurance for pediatrics was being covered.

My examining room is directly opposite the appointments desk in the clinic. I had finished with a pediatric patient and his father and asked them to come for a revisit in two weeks. I heard the appointments manager ask if the father would like to have the boy's usual doctor see him next time and I heard the father say, "No, I think we'd like to see the old guy again." After they left, the appointment lady burst out laughing, asking me to come to the desk so she could repeat what the father said. Having already heard the conversation, I was laughing, too. I figured that I had not yet completely lost my touch.

In the News

Since coming to Delaware, my public silhouette has increased somewhat. I have managed to be profiled on Philadelphia TV about seasonal allergies and featured on the entire front page of our local newspaper health section discussing food allergies. All the press people I have dealt with have been very pleasant and, to my surprise, extremely well prepared as shown by the questions they ask.

Miscellaneous

Antihistamines

My partner of many years studied at a medical school where his uncle was a distinguished professor. As a resident, he had expressed an interest in studying Allergy as a specialty. About this time, the first good antihistamine medication came on the market, the first drug to treat hayfever adequately. My partner's uncle called him into his office one day to explain to him that, with the advent of antihistamines, there would be no need for a specialty in Allergy and that his nephew ought to rethink his interest in this field. Well, my partner shortly decided to continue with his interest and the rest, as we say, is history. I'm glad he did since he asked me to come to work for him out of his residency program in Allergy and Immunology. Shortly thereafter he offered me a partnership arrangement—one that I couldn't refuse. Thus began a twenty-five year relationship for the good of a great many allergy and asthma sufferers and for us.

Please Remit

One of my favorite stories about my partner occurred when he and his wife contributed to the UJA (United Jewish Appeal), using stocks, having considered their value at the time of the gift. About eight months later, they received a bill from the UJA asking them to remit the difference between the value of the stock that they had contributed and its value later on when the price had dropped. That was the last time they gave to that particular charity!

The Grandbaby

We had been happily awaiting my partner's first grandbaby. I came into the office one morning and my partner, who was Jewish, motioned me into his office to announce that a new granddaughter had arrived. Her name? Emily Woodall Brown. His comment? "How's that for a Jewish name?"

A Small Package

For several years, my oldest son and his family lived in Lagos, Nigeria. One of the medicines he and his family needed to take while there was very expensive, unbeknown to Bill since ExxonMobil was paying for it. It had been ordered and he went to pick it up at the large, modern pharmacy in the local supermarket. The pharmacist put this tiny box on the counter and Bill took it to the checkout line. When he saw the price he was astounded, as was, apparently, the customer behind him in the line. This gentleman took one look at the register and the package and said, "What you got there?" This has become the way our family reacts to unusual events. My son-in-law, however, would explain these things as "trickery, all trickery". This is now another family saying.

The Proposal

One day, I found myself alone in the living room of my girlfriend's house. Her father was alone in the dining room and her sister and her mother were in the kitchen. I had been on notice that I would have to ask for Peggy's hand in marriage and I suddenly realized that now must be the time. I went in to Peggy's father and asked for his blessing. He questioned me about a few things and then said, quite unexpectedly I thought, though I should have been prepared to answer, "How do you propose to support my daughter?" I was dumbfounded. I replied, "I have no intention of supporting your daughter!" (Peggy and I had agreed that she would continue to work in Rochester to support us.) Mr. Cunningham was not pleased although he did give his consent to our marriage, whether conditionally or not we will never know.

The next thing I knew, he and my father arranged to go out to lunch to discuss the pending union of their children. (Prior to this from the time I started college my father sent a $25.00 check every week for me to live on as well as paying the usual college and medical school expenses.) The upshot of the lunch conference was that neither of these gentlemen was prepared to help us financially! And not only that, but after our wedding the weekly support check stopped as did the payment of my medical school expenses save for some inexplicable reason, money for my books.

Undaunted, we had a lovely wedding after a year's engagement and moved to our garret apartment in Rochester right behind St. Mary's Hospital which was a teaching venue for me. We had a wonderful time with all the other poor students, annually winning the cheapest apartment competition.

And then, in November, 1959, our first son was born. A week later arrived in the mail a check for $25.00 from my father. That continued until I graduated from medical school.

Eventually, I did have to borrow a small sum of money to pay my tuition, but it did not become a burden as so many educational loans do today.

Apollo 14

Very late one night my bedside phone rang. Of course, I assumed that it was a patient calling so I was surprised to hear one of my best college and medical school friends on the line. He immediately asked what my government clearance was. I had been out of the service for a while but I informed him that it had been "for your eyes only". (He didn't really need this information.) My friend is an obstetrician in Houston and we referred to him as "Obstetrician to the Astronauts" because he saw so many of the astronauts' wives. It seems that Dr. Charles Berry, chief NASA physician, had invited my friend and his wife to watch the Apollo 14 launch and indicated that they could invite another couple to accompany them.

We left quickly for Ft. Lauderdale and arrived at Cape Canaveral the next day. Talk about VIP treatment! We were in the company of such notables as the King and Queen of Spain and Vice President Spiro Agnew. Watching the launch from the VIP stands was beyond exciting. We partied with our friends, Dr. Berry and some of the astronauts. Dr. Berry sent pictures of the moon landing to my children who kept them on their walls for many years. It was a fondly remembered, whirlwind trip for us.

Penis Stories

My good friend George was given to announcing things at inopportune moments, usually while I was driving the car. After his successful radical prostatectomy which had rendered him impotent, he decided to have a penile implant. This turned out to be highly successful as well. While we were riding along one day, he announced out of the blue that he was going to see his urologist the following week. I asked him why that was. It seemed that every time he crossed his legs, right leg over left, he got an erection. Luckily I knew enough about these things to know that the mechanism included a small pump in the scrotum. I asked him if he understood that the doctor was going to tell him to not cross his legs that way and thus produce a cure. He did, but he wanted to make sure anyway.

Once, on the medical ward during my training, a male patient took me aside to ask me what I thought the outcome would be with his soon to be wife because of his large penis. It was indeed large. I was tempted to ask what he thought his new wife's initial reaction to seeing this appendage might be, but I refrained. Instead, I told him to take things easy, and mentioned a few things that might make things go more smoothly. I knew that eventually she would be able to accommodate him quite well without discomfort. Unfortunately, there was no way I would ever discover the outcome of my advice.

At the Medical Center for Federal Prisoners, the medical staff took turns doing the physical exams on the incoming inmates. The standard procedure was to have the prisoner strip naked and then undergo his exam. One day, a very well endowed prisoner took off his white coveralls and stood just behind and to one side of me while I did his paperwork at my desk. He was facing directly into the entrance to the hallway. I saw one of our surgeons walk past, and then, literally, back up to the entranceway and say, "Is that thing always that big?" The inmate's answer was one of the best comebacks I have ever heard. He simply said, "No." It was hard for me to keep a straight face at that point. Thereafter, I always nodded in agreement whenever someone would say that, for the most part, criminals aren't stupid.

When our third son was born, I decided for reasons unknown to me now, that he should not be circumcised. Our pediatrician called one day shortly after Christopher came home from the hospital to be sure that we had really made this decision. His final attempt at talking me into it was, "I can get you a good Rabbi!" We have always laughed over this. However, several months later it became obvious that our new baby boy had phimosis and required circumcision. Another time I did not have the last laugh.

Ophthalmologists

A good friend of mine, a general surgeon with whom I had done all my post-graduate training, was hit in the eye by a racquetball. At the time, we had both been in practice for several years. He was taken immediately to Manhattan Eye and Ear Hospital where his head was immobilized. Then began a long parade of doctors who were interested in his eye, mainly to see if it might be going to survive the injury. It did. Later on because so many doctors had come to examine his eyes, he remarked that he knew that there were specialists for the retina, doctors for the lens and various eye inflammations, but he never suspected that there were separate specialists for the right eye and for the left eye, too.

A Cactus

It seems that I was always at the dentist's office near my hospital on the west side of Seventh Avenue and the south side of 57th Street. Directly across the Avenue there was an apartment building in which a large cactus could be seen in a window. The top of the plant eventually disappeared above the window, and, to my amazement, reappeared quite some time later in the window of the apartment above. My dentist was able to verify that there was a hole for the cactus to grow through into the apartment above. Many New Yorkers buy adjacent apartments to enlarge their living spaces, so that the cactus owners may have owned the second apartment. It was a constant source of amusement for the patients. I had finished training before the cactus grew into third apartment, if it ever did.

Sal S.

Eventually I got around to seeing Sal S. about my investments. By then I had accumulated enough assets to fit on the smallest piece of paper imaginable. At the same time, I was embarrassed about going to see an "investment guy". I thought it was awfully amusing as well. So, I arrived in his office in lower Manhattan and was immediately overcome with the decor, lavish but subdued.

And so we met. After some small talk, I produced my miniscule list and asked what I should do about it. Mr. S. could not have been kinder to me, indicating that already I had some monetary worth and he would help me increase that. He called for someone to bring him several investment folders of actual clients of his which he showed to me after carefully seeing to it that I could not discover their names. Several had started with next to nothing and were now, to my way of thinking, "in the chips". There were several rules I was to follow to achieve a similar result and I did so from then on. Just before one of the mini-crashes in the eighties, I noticed that my portfolio had suddenly become mostly cash. That smart move resulted in far smaller losses for me than for others whom I knew. Now retired, sort of, and living off of those investments, I still keep most of my modest holdings with Mr. S.'s company. Mr. S. died not long ago when he was well into his nineties. I remember him well even though I rarely met him save at occasional social functions

Another very important person in my financial life was Jess B. I had set up a Keogh account with him, the first accountant I ever dealt with. One day he called to remind me to make my contribution, in those days, before March 15th. And just how I asked was I supposed to come up with so much cash since at the time I was using all my income just to put food on the table. He insisted that I borrow the funds from the bank, which I did in a state of disbelief. About three years later, I was finally able to fund the account without borrowing anything. When I think of it now, he did me a terrific service, the money I borrowed so many years ago having grown substantially because of its long history of compounded interest. My current advisor, whom I met while attending one of his classes, has become a good friend and excellent financial advisor. Though he lives in Greenwich Village in New York City, he is a member of the Popcorn Club.

The Sale

A long-time friend of mine and an internationally known allergist told me that he was going to make an offer to purchase my practice. He had actually mentioned this several years earlier as we two couples sat at a table on the River Walk in San Antonio. The most appealing part of this idea beyond the fact of our friendship was that he wanted to buy both parts of my practice. I had already been approached about selling the city and the suburban parts separately which I didn't want to do. In addition, his Manhattan office was one block from my office in Manhattan and he would be using my office in White Plains. Thus, patients would not be inconvenienced by my leaving.

I took Ira's offer to my accountant, who, unbeknown to me, had overseen several practice sales, to see what he thought of the sale terms. Peggy and I were very nervous about this and became even more so when the accountant took such a long time to comment on the terms. Finally, I blurted out that I would be able to have the prospective buyer come to a meeting with him if necessary. Suddenly he burst out laughing, saying that he was not interested in meeting with Ira since he didn't want to have to tell him what a good deal he was offering me. Understandably this was a great relief to Peggy and me. Negotiations with my friend went easily after that and the deal was concluded. (When word got out, other doctors began calling to try, without my knowledge, to hire my office staff. The staff all thought it was very funny and Ira had already agreed to continue to have them work for him. I, on the other hand, was not amused.) Besides, I had to convince the new employer that I paid them as well as I did because they were all of great value to the practice. At least one of those people continues to work for the practice twelve years later and another retired after she had worked another seven years after I left. My New York City office manager went to nursing school. These developments pleased me very much and everyone was quite satisfied with the deal.

The Telephone Man

A friend of mine in training and his wife were naturists, in their own home so far as I know. They had just moved to a new apartment when the telephone man came to hook up the phones. They always kept robes near the door to put on when necessary. However, this day their two little boys were playing without clothes in the house. They were shooed quickly into the closet near the front door and the telephone man came in. He searched all over the apartment to find the telephone lines he needed to make the connections but was unable to find them. Finally he said that often they were in a closet. Whereupon he opened the front door closet and out ran two naked little boys! Of course, the doctor's wife was mortified, but the installer took it all in stride. Later on I learned from a man who had done installation work in homes that the best part of his job was never knowing what was going to happen when he worked in someone else's house.

The Last Laugh

I told my best friend, Lou, that we were going to have a baby. We already had two boys and a girl—our youngest child at the time was 8 years old. I can still remember how Lou laughed over that. Lou had three girls by then, the youngest about 12 years old. Shortly after our Christopher arrived, Lou told me one day that he and Stella were going to have another baby. Neither one of us could figure out how these things had come about, but, boy, did I have the last laugh, at Lou's expense this time.

The Weather Report

While we were driving through South Carolina one warm summer day, the weather lady came on the radio. She gave the current statistics and then said, "And tonight it will be dark!" My wife and I looked at each other and burst out laughing. No doubt that was the lady's last day of work and she was having some fun on her way out. I did not pull anything like that when I retired from practice.

Reflections

The Practice of Medicine

In general, the education of doctors in pre-med is lacking. The quality of the courses they take before medical school is, or ought to be, excellent. The problem is with the pre-med curriculum. By the time many pre-med students are college seniors, there is little else that they are able to do but to continue on to medical school. So, while much is made of having a well-rounded education in college, this often turns out not to be the case. In my class in medical school, we had one student who did not have a college degree of any sort, and another who was an expert in Elizabethan literature. Both very learned people who seemed well prepared for medical studies. Most of the rest of us had a college education in general science with an emphasis on biology and chemistry. Since the first most important academic course in medical school was biochemistry, mastering that course alone might have been sufficient to allow some college science courses to be to be taken instead in general education; English, literature, the arts, history, etc. I think by now that may often be the case. One can hope.

Medical Student Behavior

Recently there have been reports of bad behavior by medical students on the Internet. These often take place in the social contact websites. Some schools are putting out guidelines for internet behavior to their students. As one medical facility doctor noted, outrageous behavior by medical students has been around much longer than the internet, but really should be kept under control. My medical school class approached bad taste on one occasion in a parody of some of our medical school activities. It got rave reviews from students and professors, however. The main problem concerned how to keep the grapefruit attached to "Mrs. Cumming", whom I had the great good fortune to portray. But, in my medical school at least, there were very strict rules of behavior in force which we followed quite conscientiously.

A Learning Experience

Many years ago an old friend of mine underwent a radical mastectomy. She did well even in the days before chemotherapy and radiation. Eventually, however, she needed to have her other breast removed as well. By then additional treatments were also employed. When she was about 80 years old she required a pacemaker. In the hospital, the young doctor arrived to measure her for the device. He finally settled on a location for it and was preparing to leave, when my friend asked if he had any idea what her prosthesis was like for her to wear. He admitted that he did not, so my friend's daughter brought it out from the closet. He was floored by its weight and size and knew immediately that a new measuring job was required for the pacemaker placement. He also allowed as how my friend had taught him an important lesson, one which his professors had not and one that he would never forget while preparing patients for surgery, especially when mechanical devices and incisions were involved. My friend is now about 92, doing just fine and wearing her prosthesis quite comfortably.

Primadonnas

Many physicians fancy themselves to be more important than they really are. This can lead to their being insensitive. One such physician, a pediatrician, encountered my wife in the hospital where she was visiting with our son before his operation for a hip disorder. We knew that this was a serious condition, requiring him to have a pin placed in his upper leg bone. I knew that it often developed in the opposite leg also, but my wife did not. The doctor asked why Billy was there, announced that the condition would probably be repeated in the other leg, and left the room. This left my son startled and my wife furious with the doctor for having upset both of them unnecessarily. Fortunately, he did not require another operation but was left with one tiny bit shorter leg.

On the other hand, many doctors give freely of their time to help in educating the public medically. A case in point was a local cardiologist who spoke to our Rotary Club about the signs and symptoms of a heart attack. One club member at lunch that day began to experience some of the symptoms described the next morning while he was still in bed after his wife had left for work. A review in his mind of what he had heard the day before caused him to call a neighbor for help. The Club member, another old friend of mine, was transported to the hospital not far away. He had cardiac arrest in the Emergency Room, was resuscitated and treated successfully with the methods then current. Today, he is in his mid-eighties, still playing golf and I'm sure still thankful for the good doctor at the Rotary lunch.

Teaching Aids

Remembering the names of things and how they work is important in any learning situation. Here are a few things I learned in medical school:

The Boxcar Theory—Bowel function, especially in the large intestine was easier to picture as peristalsis caused by one" boxcar" after another being propelled along the intestinal tract.

Parasitology Pearl—One studies the mite bite site of the house mouse louse.

Wrist Bones—Never Lower Tillie's Pants, Mother Might Come Home. (Navicular, Lunate, etc.)

Cranial Nerves—On Old Olympus' Towering Top A Finn And German Viewed A Hop. (Olfactory, Optic, etc.)

The tincture of time—on letting things improve by themselves.

The first rule of medicine—If what you are doing is working, keep doing it.

The two most alarming words in medicine—Oh, oh.

Keeping Secrets

Very early in my career I learned that it is nearly impossible to keep an illness secret.

One evening at a dinner party a high school classmate of mine, by now a prominent lawyer in town and our host, made a cryptic comment to another guest, also a classmate of mine and now a well-known physician, about his, the lawyer's, health. I knew he had been under the weather but no one had any idea how sick he really was. Shortly thereafter, I happened to see his wife standing under the New York Hospital sign while I was travelling south on the IRT subway. Right then, I knew that my friend was seriously ill. After he died, I was informed by several people and by way of a newspaper article that no one in our town knew about his illness except for his wife and the other doctor at the dinner party. I had kept my suspicions to myself and no one knew how and why I had figured things out. He died at age 32 of Hodgkin's Disease, almost certainly curable today.

Another time after I had parked my car near The Roosevelt Hospital very early in the morning, I practically bumped into a good friend and former patient just outside the Janeway Cancer Treatment Center. To my question about what he was doing there on the street, I got a vague answer about meeting a client. I didn't put two and two together until about two weeks later when I spotted my friend at the same time in the same place. He didn't see me and I made sure he didn't, but I knew then that there was a problem. He died a few months later in his forties from a brain tumor. No one in town supposedly knew about his illness and I was not about to inform anyone otherwise.

The moral, I guess, is that keeping such information secret is not likely to work very well and makes it less likely that the patient will be able to benefit from an active support group.

Placement Tests

I think it was sometime around sixth grade that we took standardized placement tests, I suppose to see what sorts of occupations we might be suited for. I would do best as a secretary or a bus driver! I thought this was funny then and I still do of course, but my father, a school teacher, was horrified. The test results were wrong but I am a little compulsive about paperwork and could probably drive a bus if I had to.

In high school, I took Journalism and fourth year English at the same time and scored well in English on the New York State Regents Exam. I also took German 2 and 3 at the same time, doing well on both Regents exams. So I just knew I would be placed well beyond beginning level in these two subjects in college. Who knew? I landed in English 1-2 where my instructor complained that my writing style was too much like the "inverted triangle" used in newspaper reporting where the most important facts are put at the beginning of the article, becoming less important as the piece unfolded. But, I was placed in Advanced German Literature. Here I was in real trouble almost immediately. I was not alone. Fortunately, we had a kindly professor who made things as easy as he could for us. Even when I had to write my final semester exam entirely in German, I somehow muddled through.

The Grave Site

Since, according to a little old lady I used to care for, "more people are dying now than have ever died before", my wife and I finally purchased a grave site in Dover, DE. My wife keeps a sign in the laundry room which says. "It's Not Easy Being a Queen". At the cemetery we found a nice location for our grave. We then realized that it was on the corner of William Street and Queen Street. We were particularly amused by the reaction of our son since he will be passing this location frequently in his patrol car. My wife's comment about the fact that we will be buried one atop the other is TMI according to the kids.

Pet Peeves

Some people are so adept at disguising how unintelligent they really are that I get annoyed, mostly with myself, for not figuring this out quickly. With one patient, her lack of intelligence hit me one day while I was treating her. I mentioned this to my secretary who had no idea that I hadn't known this as long as she had.

Some things people tell me also bother me. An example is the lady who announced at the outset of her initial visit that her dog did not bother her since it had "human hair"! I had to invent a non-peevish response to this on the spot.

And then there is, "Why didn't you come for your visit last week?" "I was too sick to go to the doctor!"

Friends who are patients sometimes call me at home with a medical problem, and then complain that they couldn't reach me. Well, of course they couldn't since I wasn't there. I explain as gently as I can that they should call the answering service which will always be able to find me.

I don't pretend to have a great fund of knowledge outside of my field, but I do know when I am hearing statements of "fact" that are just plain nonsense. For the most part I have learned to keep my mouth shut when this happens, but occasionally I hear misinformation that actually could be harmful and then I speak up, as tactfully as I can.

"No shows" are patients who have appointments but don't come in and don't cancel the appointment. This was rarely a problem before I retired but is quite prevalent where I am now. Attempts to reach these people or to charge a fee for these missed appointments largely fail.

"Allergy" can be a sort of dumping ground for patients' problems which are difficult to diagnose, and irritates me when I am expected to treat things like Alzheimer's Disease, all manner of odd food intolerances and a whole range of non-allergic skin diseases. However, in fact, my career blossomed after I sent a patient back to the ENT doctor who sent her to me because he could not tell what was wrong with her and it had to be "allergic". He had an enormous practice in town and had never sent me a patient before. So I did all the usual things including skin testing, and I could not find anything wrong which could be attributed to allergy. I was quite disappointed when I sent her back to the ENT doctor with negative findings. I could have easily said that she needed allergy shots, but I never did business that way. He called a few days later, told me that he had reexamined the patient and had found an anatomical abnormality that he missed initially. He complimented me on my diagnostic honesty and from then on sent all of his allergy work to me. A real coup for me.

Other problems include not receiving reports from physicians I have sent to other doctors, being called down because of the oral cortisone medications I need to use in higher doses than referring physicians would prefer, and having repeatedly to reeducate emergency room doctors on the correct treatment for allergic, sometimes life-threatening, emergencies

A Future Physician

Just the other day I looked up from writing some instructions for her mother and saw my five year old ("I'm almost six!") patient with my stethoscope in her ears, placed correctly. As I went back to my writing, I felt my stethoscope pressed on my back. My patient, quite emphatically, said, "Breathe!" I did as I was told, as noisily as I could so that she would hear something through my clothes. When she was done with her exam, I asked her if she was going to be a doctor. "Probably," she replied and went off to get her lollipop. Who knows, maybe someday she'll write some tales about her life in medicine.

LaVergne, TN USA
04 March 2010
174989LV00001B/200/P